The Prayer Book Tradition
in the Free Churches

A. Elliott Peaston

Former minister in Dromore
Unitarian Church.

with a Foreword by
Edward C. Ratcliff

(L)

The Lutterworth Press
Cambridge

Published by
The Lutterworth Press
P.O. Box 60
Cambridge
CB1 2NT
England

e-mail: **publishing@lutterworth.com**
website: **http://www.lutterworth.com**

ISBN 0 7188 9120 1 hardback
ISBN 0 7188 9119 8 paperback

British Library Cataloguing in Publication Data:
A catalogue record is available from the British Library.

First published 1964 by James Clarke & Co.
Reprinted 2002

CONTENTS

ACKNOWLEDGEMENTS

IT would not be possible for the writer to acknowledge by name the many scholars and divines to whom he is under obligation for gracious help. Some of them, such as Dr. Hensley Henson and Dr. Orchard, are no longer with us, to our great loss. It is said of the Venerable Bede that he would not that a lie should appear in his book. If the writer has managed to relate, with the accuracy he would desire, the liturgical histories of the Free Churches it is because of invaluable information generously given.

Perhaps he may be pardoned for an expression of especial gratitude to Mr. Robert Wilkinson, M.B.E., of Belfast, to Mr. A. Doloughan, of Dromore, Co. Down, and to the Reverend P. N. Tindall, M.A., B.D., Ph.D. The tedious task of proof-reading was undertaken by them.

Nor would he forego an opportunity of expressing filial devotion to the Hibbert Trustees and the Dr. Daniel Jones Trustees. A truly paternal benevolence has been theirs.

Finally, as on a previous occasion, the writer would record his indebtedness to the Reverend Professor Edward C. Ratcliff. Without his inspiring interest this book would neither have been completed, nor contemplated.

FOREWORD

By the Regius Professor of Divinity in the University of Cambridge

IT is no small honour to be invited by Mr. Peaston to contribute a Foreword to his book. If I accept his invitation with pleasure, I accept it also as in a certain 'private duty bound'. In the respective capacities of examinee and examiner, Mr. Peaston and I first made acquaintance with each other at Oxford nearly a quarter century ago. On reading the examinee's thesis, the examiner was left in no doubt that the examinee had made himself an authority in a hitherto unexplored field of English liturgical study. The title of the thesis, published in 1940, was *The Prayer Book Reform Movement in the XVIIIth Century.* The Movement, though stimulated from within the Established Church, had its effect outside; and the forms of revision, to which the Movement gave rise, constituted material for an interesting and significant, if extra-Anglican, chapter in Prayer Book History. What of other revisions and adaptations of the Prayer Book, not proceeding from official Anglican initiative, and undertaken before and after the eighteenth century? Mr. Peaston's thesis inevitably provoked the question. It was equally inevitable to suggest that Mr. Peaston should embark upon the inquiry. No other, indeed, had shown himself qualified to do so.

At last, after many years of arduous research, and not without hindrance and discouragement on the way, Mr. Peaston has completed his larger inquiry, and *The Prayer Book Tradition in the Free Churches* is now before us. Mr. Peaston begins with the Marian emigrants and their treatment of the Prayer Book in their congregations on the Continent. Turning next to the Elizabethan Puritans, he finds *inter alia* interesting material in revisions of the Prayer Book incorporated in Geneva Bibles. So far the student of Prayer Book history may not be treading on wholly unfamiliar ground, but he will quickly discover that

Mr. Peaston has more to teach him than he expected. When he
follows Mr. Peaston's examination of the Puritan tradition as
it survived in Methodism, in the Countess of Huntingdon's
Connexion, and in the Free Church of England, he moves into
new territory which is more interesting than he may have
suspected. Not less deserving of attention are the uses made of
the Prayer Book by the Moravians, the Congregationalists, the
Baptists, and the Churches of Christ. These last, whom Mr.
Peaston broadly treats as 'Orthodox', are the subject of the
second part of his book. The third part is devoted to the
'Heterodox' tradition, and is concerned with the 'New' or
Swedenborgian Church; it contains much that will surprise the
liturgist. In his final short part, Mr. Peaston deals with the
'Catholic' tradition as represented by the 'Catholic Apostolic
Church' associated with the name of Edward Irving, and also
by the 'Free Catholic Society', of which, at the beginning of
the present century, Dr. W. E. Orchard and the Reverend
Lloyd Thomas were the well-known leaders. The Catholic
Apostolic prayer book, *The Liturgy and other Divine Offices of the
Church*, has never received the notice which it merits, probably
because copies of it were difficult to come by. On this account,
Mr. Peaston's examination of it is particularly welcome.

It is no exaggeration to say that Mr. Peaston has completed
the extra-Anglican history of the Prayer Book. In so doing, he
has done more; he has made a notable contribution to the
history of English religion. The life of a Church is in its worship;
and to students who wish to penetrate beneath the sometimes
strange exteriors of the English Free Churches to the spirit
which has animated them, Mr. Peaston furnishes indispensable
guidance. His book is the work of a master. It is a pleasure and
an honour to commend it.

EDWARD C. RATCLIFF

St. John's College,
   Cambridge.
15th March 1963

PREFACE

IT is an assumption commonly made that liturgical worship is confined to the older Communions in the Catholic tradition. It is understood that the Free Churches of England adhere to 'free services'. Such an assumption is no longer valid. Liturgical interest has revived in England, and many Free Churchmen are experimenting with liturgical forms. A scholarly interest in liturgiology is a somewhat new phenomenon in the Free Churches, but it would be wrong to assume that liturgical worship as such is of recent origin. It is the purpose of this book to trace the development of liturgical worship in those Communions always regarded as belonging to the strict Protestant tradition.

At the Reformation the Church of England remained faithful to liturgical worship. The Elizabethan settlement was a statesmanlike compromise, and Elizabeth hoped that the Book of Common Prayer would prove acceptable to all her subjects. The devotion of many Englishmen to the Prayer Book went far to justify this hope. But the more extreme Catholics proved intractable, and the more extreme Protestants remained restive.

Since the time of the great Queen, periodic attempts have been made to amend the Prayer Book, and many suggested revisions have been forthcoming. It is not the purpose of this book to deal with the more conservative and Catholic revisions. These have received the attention of scholars. Rather is it the design of this study to deal with the more radical and Protestant revisions, not only because they are not so well known, but because they are the parent of much liturgical revision in the Free Churches. It will be seen that reforms suggested by Puritans and seventeenth-century Presbyterians have frequently found their way into Free Church prayer books.

Some of the Free Churches came to develop distinctive points of theology of their own. It is the further aim of this study to show how English Nonconformists not only inherited

I

Puritan ideas but even revised the Prayer Book to suit their own peculiar tenets of belief. They were not to remain content with this. As time passed and the Free Churches became increasingly strong, the influence of the Church of England and the Prayer Book began to wane. Henceforth the Nonconformists began to produce prayer books of their own, independent of the Anglican tradition. Some of these effusions were, to say the least, unfortunate. But they cannot be ignored. They remain part of the religious heritage of England.

The Prayer Book tradition in the Free Churches had its beginnings among those zealous Puritans who sought to purge the Prayer Book of Romanism. Rites and ceremonies became suspect, and doctrines not authorised by the Holy Scriptures anathema. Events proved that the Church of England was not prepared to become Puritan. But the tradition itself did not die. It survived to bloom anew in the Free Churches.

The Free Churches remained staunchly Protestant. But by the close of the nineteenth century they had lost much of their old dread of the Bishop of Rome. Moreover, Anglicans and Free Churchmen were entering upon a new and happier relationship. Already had the Romantic Movement restored to Englishmen the lost enchantments of the Middle Ages, so that even Free Churchmen were beginning to build Gothic churches.

It is not to be supposed that the Free Churches would countenance an Oxford Movement. But Free Churchmen have shown an increasing appreciation of liturgical tradition, and an increasing disposition to make use of prayers from pre-Reformation sources. Thus the most recent Congregational prayer book, *A Book of Services and Prayers*, contains 'A Treasury of Prayers from ancient Liturgies'.

Occasionally the enthusiasm of individual Free Churchmen for the ancient Catholic piety has given rise to services of a pronounced Catholic character. These are of interest to the liturgist, though they are in truth side-streams only. The remarkable thing is that they should have come into existence at all. Only the revived interest in liturgiology among Free Churchmen will explain it.

Paradoxically, therefore, this book is to end with a brief description of the emergence of Catholic rites and practices in the Free Churches. But the 'Catholic Apostolic Church' is dying, and the Society of Free Catholics is defunct.

An examination of Free Church liturgical history would seem to suggest the emergence of four main traditions—hence the division of this book into as many parts. This classification cuts across the strict denominational frontiers. But as each denomination maintains a separate, corporate existence, it is treated separately, though grouped with others in a like tradition. Thus the small, but historically interesting, Countess of Huntingdon's Connexion has many links with Methodism. But it is not part of the Methodist Church.

Again, the four traditions do not exist in isolation. They are more like threads which at times are intertwined. Thus, the Moravians, though not in the Anglican tradition, have bishops of their own, and have enjoyed, at various times, close fellowship with the Church of England. Despite these confusions the traditions are real and not arbitrary.

The Methodists (more especially the Wesleyan Methodists) are self-confessedly in the Anglican Tradition. So is the Free Church of England, which lays claim to the historic episcopate. Their revisions of the Book of Common Prayer are Puritan in temper and often in design. They may be understood only by reference to the English Puritans of the sixteenth and seventeenth centuries. That is why this book begins with the extremely important revisions of the Marian exiles and the Elizabethan Puritans. The liturgical activities of the Elizabethan Puritans, so surreptitious and tortuous, are examined in detail for the first time.

The Moravians, the Congregationalists, the Baptists and Churches of Christ are treated as belonging to the Dissenting tradition. Their liturgical tradition is not Anglican, though influenced by it. The Moravian Church has its roots in fifteenth-century Bohemia, and an attempt is made to indicate the influence of this long history on the British Province of the Church. This arose in England in the eighteenth century. It was then that the Moravians made so profound an impression on John Wesley.

The Congregationalists are the heirs of the Independents who rejected the imposition by the State of a uniform liturgy. But modern Congregationalists are taking an increasing interest in

3

liturgiology. That this is not an entirely new departure the chapter on the Congregationalists is designed to show. For a hundred years individual Congregationalists have experimented with some sort of liturgical worship.

Not so the Baptists, who have shown little affection for liturgies. But perhaps it is a sign of the times that of late they have made tentative moves in a liturgical direction.

It will be observed that no account is given in this book of the liturgical publications of the Presbyterian Church of England. This Church has very close affinities with Scotland. Thus *The Presbyterian Service Book for use in the Presbyterian Churches of England and Wales* (1948) makes use of Scottish sources. This book is a great advance on a previous book, *The Directory of Public Worship* (published in 1898, and revised in 1921). These books more properly belong to a study of Scottish liturgy.

The third tradition is frankly heterodox. New Church liturgies are of interest because of the determination of the followers of Emanuel Swedenborg to preserve liturgical worship. At times the influence of the Anglican tradition is evident, and these liturgies contain some interesting revisions of Prayer Book services.

A study of Semi-Arian and Unitarian Prayer Book revisions may be found in a previous book.

Somewhat remarkably this analysis concludes with the Catholic tradition. It would appear to be abortive, though Dr. Orchard is still of interest to many people, and the fine liturgy of the 'Catholic Apostolic Church' has received the encomium of scholars.

The truth is that interest in liturgiology would seem to be on the increase in the Free Churches of England. An old love of the Prayer Book still haunts the heirs of the Dissenters. At a time when prayers are being offered for the unity of Christendom, it may be of service to show how general is the desire of Christian people to make of public worship something true and lovely.

PART I

The Anglican Tradition

CHAPTER I

THE GENESIS OF PRAYER BOOK
WORSHIP IN ENGLISH NONCONFORMITY

THE Book of Common Prayer is the greatest gift the Church of England has bestowed on the English-speaking world. No longer is it the exclusive possession of a national Church. In the twentieth century the far-flung Anglican communion is linked, in the English way, by loyalty to a venerable tradition and love for an ancient piety. The Prayer Book is typical of England even in this. It has crossed the seven seas. Nor is this all. Historic Nonconformity forsook the Mother Church and repudiated her liturgy. But the Free Churches, with a fine English scorn for mere consistency, have shown an inclination to sanction forms of prayer and modifications of the Prayer Book.

The fact is that Cranmer's masterpiece makes an appeal to English hearts, irrespective of creed or sect. Thomas Hardy, whose philosophy of life was scarcely at one with Christian orthodoxy, attended his parish church. 'The Liturgy of the Church of England', he wrote, 'is a noble thing. So are Tate and Brady's Psalms. These are the things that people need and should have.'

The Protestant reformers, who directed the course of the Reformation under the boy-King Edward VI, were not blind to the exceptional merits of their book. But a liturgy is something more than a manual of devotion. It is a rule of faith. Soon radical Protestants were at variance with their more reactionary brethren. The First Prayer Book of Edward VI (1549) was conservative in tone and Catholic in spirit, being in many ways a very close approximation to the Sarum Breviary, Missal, and Manual. The fall of the Protector Somerset and the rise to power of a new Protector, Northumberland, prepared the way for further change. By an Act of Parliament of April 1552, the Second Prayer Book of Edward VI replaced the First. Vestments were forbidden, save for rochet and surplice. The altar gave place to a communion table standing 'in the body of the Church, or in the chancel'. A black rubric was appended to the Communion Service. Unction disappeared from the Visitation of the Sick and prayers for the departed from the Burial of the Dead.

Already those features were appearing that were to be characteristic of Puritanism and Evangelicalism. Prominent among them was an abhorrence of Romanism, and a conviction, often frankly expressed, that the pope was Antichrist. The Litany in the Second Prayer Book gives fierce expression to this view: 'from the tyranny of the Bishop of Rome, and all his detestable enormities. . . . Good Lord, deliver us.' Such language has a strange sound for modern ears. But the insinuation of rites and doctrine unknown to Holy Writ was explained by the craft of the false Vicar of Christ. Not Papal Infallibility but Biblical Infallibity was the cardinal tenet of Puritans as of Evangelicals ever since. Many held that the validity of Christian worship must be attested by Scripture rule, and nothing unauthorised by Scripture allowed in a godly prayer book.

But it would be wrong to suppose that the divines responsible for King Edward's Second Book were extremists. Puritanism hardened with the advance of Protestantism. Nor do men, even the most conscientious, always act consistently. The Second Prayer Book was intolerant of some ceremonies only. 'But what would S. Augustine have said,' demands this book, 'if he had seen the ceremonies of late days used among us? . . . This our excessive multitude of ceremonies was so great, and many of them so dark, that they did more confound, and darken, than declare and set forth Christ's benefits unto us.' But not all ceremonies were harmful. A seemly law and order must be observed, and some ceremonies retained. 'Others there be, which although they have been devised by man, yet it is thought good to reserve them still, as well for a decent order in the church (for the which they were first devised) as because they pertain to edification.' But it was precisely this assumption that many later Puritans could not make. The use of the surplice, the cross in baptism, the ring in marriage, and kneeling at Communion, all sanctioned by Edward's Second Book, became intolerable as relics of a hateful Romanism.

The Second Prayer Book of Edward VI came into legal effect on 1st November 1552. It is certain it was never in general use or widely known. On 6th July 1553, Edward VI died. Prayer Book and Protestantism alike were swept away by the Catholic revival of Mary. But Edward's Second Book was not stillborn. It was to be restored, with a few very significant changes, under Elizabeth. Even before this, however, it was to have a strange, adventurous career, first on the Continent, and then in Scotland, where for a few years it became the official liturgy of the Kirk.

The accession of Mary was the signal for flight abroad of hundreds of uncompromising Protestants. Congregations were formed in Germany and Switzerland by zealous members of the Cranmer party. These exiles faithfully preserved and observed the Second Prayer Book. Soon this devotion was challenged.

During Edward's reign, the Protestant pastor Vallerand Pullain and his small Walloon congregation had been permitted to worship in the disused abbey of Glastonbury. A change of abode being necessary on Edward's death, they found another refuge at Frankfort-on-the-Main and another place of worship at the famous Cistercian or White Ladies' Church, a picturesque building reduced by the Second World War to bare grim-looking walls. Even in England Pullain had used not the English Book but a reformed Continental service. This he had translated into Latin and dedicated to King Edward. In June 1554, four groups of English refugees, including the famous William Whittingham, a future Dean of Durham, arrived in Frankfort. They were given a warm welcome by Pullain and permission by the civic authorities to share the Church of the White Ladies, providing they 'should not dissent from the Frenchmen in doctrine or ceremonies, lest they should thereby minister occasion of offence'. This assurance they were very willing to give. Already some of the more extreme Protestants in the Church of England such as Hooper and Ridley were disturbed by the rites and ceremonies still countenanced by King Edward's Second Book. Whittingham and most of his friends were anxious for a more drastic revision, or even

9

for the adoption of a liturgy of the Reformed Continental type.

It should have been possible for these Englishmen to work out their own forms of worship, in the liberty of their exile, without undue friction. But ideas of tolerance were alien to the sixteenth-century mind. Moreover one supreme consideration guided the activities of these men. All hoped for happier days when the gospel light should shine once more in England. All were determined that the Protestant restoration, when it came, should be conducted in the right way. But what was the right way? In a letter to Calvin on 23rd February 1555, Dean Sampson wrote from Strasburg: 'Some desire the Book of Reformation of the Church of England to be set aside altogether, others only deem some things in it objectionable . . . some contend for retaining the form, both because the Archbishop of Canterbury (Cranmer) defends the doctrine as sound, and also because the opposite party can assign no just reason why the form should be changed.' Here then was the dilemma, and it was never to be solved to the satisfaction of all.

The hope cherished by the exiles that they were working for the ultimate triumph of their principles in England was far removed from wishful thinking. Though numerically insignificant, these pockets of Protestantism included many famous men, and a remarkable number of past and future bishops and deans. Their belief in the importance of their disputations was not presumptuous. Nor were their bickerings and 'troubles' so scandalous as may appear in retrospect. These men were wrestling for the truth.

The Frankfort congregation, the most important of the exile groups, decided to be governed by collegiate pastors of equal authority, 'as is accustomed in the best reformed churches'. An invitation was dispatched to John Knox at Geneva to become one of the pastors. In deference to the express wish of Calvin, but with considerable reluctance, he accepted.

Already had this remarkable man known the ebb and flow of fortune. He had been a chaplain to Edward VI. He had survived nineteen months in irons on the French galleys. Now he was to undergo an experience of peculiar vexation and mortification. Knox was an austere Protestant, but he was not at this time uncompromising.

In England he had accepted the Edwardian settlement. Although an opponent of ceremonies he had come to 'think well' of Edward's Second Book, and had even advised his old congregation at Berwick to kneel at Communion, though strongly denouncing this practice in a sermon delivered before the Court at Windsor.

Knox's mind was alienated from the Prayer Book by the 'troubles' at Frankfort. He found a divided congregation. Some were extreme Calvinists whose heart was set on reform after Calvin's model. Others were deeply attached to a book they regarded as the supreme achievement of the English Reformation. After considerable difficulty a settlement was reached. In February 1555, a compromise liturgy was adopted, based upon the Second Prayer Book of Edward VI. It is significant that the first important revision of the Prayer Book was by way of omissions, rather than additions or substitutions. Future Puritan and Evangelical revisions were to follow this principle. But the compromise was short-lived.

A fresh party of exiles arrived at Frankfort in March, under the leadership of Richard Cox, a former tutor to Edward VI. Cox held moderate views with relentless inflexibility. As Cranmer's favourite liturgical assistant he was determined to save the Book of Common Prayer from the destructive reform of John Knox or anyone else. Nor was this the only issue. Cox had a deep personal distrust of the Scot. He wanted rid of him as a dangerous man. During the early months of 1554 the prisons of England had been filling with the faithful, and the lives of Protestants hung in a tremulous balance. It was a time for caution and discretion. Notwithstanding this, Knox had issued in the summer of that year what Cox and his friends afterwards described to Calvin as an 'outrageous pamphlet'. The *Faithful Admonition unto the professors of God's truth in England* denounced the approaching marriage of Philip of Spain and Mary of England in violent terms. Soon afterwards, the stake was ablaze for Protestant victims. It was generally believed that these horrors were the result of Knox's attack on the royal marriage. 'Before the publication of that book', wrote the Coxians to Calvin, 'not one of our brethren had suffered death, but as soon as it came forth, we doubt not but that you are well aware of the number of excellent men who have perished in the flames.' Fresh from these scenes of torture and torment Cox was in no mood for dispassionate discussion with the man he deemed responsible.

The new-comers insisted upon saying the responses in the Litany on Sunday morning. Knox retaliated in his sermon that afternoon. He inveighed against the superstitions of the Second Book, and the venal character of the clergy, some of whom sat before him, who had not scrupled to enjoy plural benefices in the Church, 'to the great slander of the gospel'.

A final attempt at compromise broke down because of Cox's insistence on versicles and responses at Morning and Evening Prayer. Knox refused to comply. 'If I was fervent,' he protested, 'I was fervent for God.'

Cox thereupon finished the controversy by drawing the attention of the magistrates to his antagonist's *Admonition*. Knox had compared Queen Mary to Jezebel, rather to the advantage of Jezebel. Another striking comparison of the Emperor Charles V with the Emperor Nero alarmed the city magistrates who instructed Knox to take his leave.

Knox never forgave his denouncers. No longer could he regard the Book of Common Prayer without bitterness. Arriving in Scotland in 1559 he found the English book in general use among the reformers. Now his great authority was thrown against it. In a letter to his friend Mrs. Locke in that year, he fulminates against 'these dregs of papistry which are left in your great Book of England'. Crossing in baptism, kneeling at the Lord's Table, mummelling of the Litany he assails as 'diabolical inventions'. He will have no dealings with the mingle-mangle of a bastard religion. Saints' days and the solemn days of the Christian Year, such as Good Friday, are 'papistical superstition'. Four years later, Knox was to give pointed emphasis to this conviction by his marriage to Margaret Stewart on a Palm Sunday! Events played into his hand. Mary, Queen of Scots, returned to her native land, and, as Knox put it in a letter to Calvin, 'that idol of the Mass was again set up'.

A more uncompromising Protestantism came into favour. No longer was Knox thought to be too extreme. The English ambassador reported this of him to Elizabeth's minister Throckmorton: 'He ruleth the roost, and of him all men stand in fear.' The Book of Common Prayer in Scotland was doomed. Thus the troubles at Frankfort wrecked the chances of a common liturgy for the Church of England and the Church of Scotland.

ANALYSIS OF 'THE LITURGY OF COMPROMISE' (1555)

This was the title given by Dr. Sprott to the compromise liturgy drawn up by Knox and Whittingham in conference with Lever and Parry who were moderate Anglicans. Lever had been Master of St. John's College, Cambridge, and Parry Chancellor of Salisbury. It was accepted by the congregation on 6th February 1555, and was in use till the end of April. The actual title of the manuscript in the British Museum is, 'The Order of Common Prayer. The ministration of Christ's holy Sacraments and of Christian discipline used in the English congregation at Frankfurt.'

The liturgy is a simplification, or as some would have it a mutilation, of the Second Prayer Book of Edward VI. 'It is thought profitable', declares the Preface, 'to signify unto all men, that although in the book of common prayer last set forth by the authority of King Edward of most famous memory, we neither condemn, judge, nor refuse anything as wicked or repugnant to the true sense and meaning of God's Word (which we the Pastors, Elders, and others of the learned sort in this congregation do testify by our subscription to this present). Yet notwithstanding we have omitted in respect of time, place, and such circumstances, certain rites and ceremonies appointed in the said book, as things of their own nature indifferent.'

The manuscript does not give the services in full. It is more of the nature of a draft or directory detailing the parts of the prayer book to be used. The liturgy is noteworthy because of the systematic substitution of 'minister' or 'pastor' for 'priest'. The words 'Mattins' and 'Evensong' are not used. Versicles and suffrages are retained. They were said by the minister alone until the arrival of the Coxians. So also was the Litany. The Te Deum and Benedicite remain.

The Communion Service, which is to be celebrated on the first Sunday of every month, begins with the collect for purity and the ten commandments. A prayer for the times is substituted for the collect for the sovereign. The collect, epistle, and gospel are removed. There follows the prayer 'for the whole

13

state of Christ's Church', the creed and offertory sentences. Then come the three exhortations, the brief exhortation to confession of sins, and the general confession. After this, the 'pastor' gives the absolution. This is succeeded by the comfortable words. The sursum corda, prefaces, and tersanctus are omitted. The prayer of humble access follows, and the order continues as in the Second Prayer Book. It is of interest to note that the placing of the prayer of humble access immediately after the comfortable words is an anticipation of the Deposited Book of 1928.

In the service of Public Baptism the first prayer, 'Almighty and everliving God', which contains the words 'didst sanctify ... waters' is left out. The sponsors reply for themselves, not for the child. To the question, 'Do you forsake the devil and all his works?' they reply, 'We forsake them'. The prayer, 'Almighty, everliving God' is removed. In the prayer of thanksgiving, the words, 'that it hath pleased Thee to regenerate this infant' are changed to, 'it doth please Thee to regenerate this infant'. The father of the child as well as the godparents are addressed in the final exhortation, as in other Reformed liturgies. The sign of the cross and the words referring thereto are omitted.

The form for Private Baptism, allowed by the Second Book for cases of 'great cause and necessity', is omitted. The influence of Knox is evident here, to the serious concern of Ridley. In a letter to Grindal the bishop wrote: 'As for private baptism, it is not prescribed in the book, but when solemn baptism by lack of time and danger of death cannot be had, what would he (Knox) in that case should be done? Peradventure he will say, it is better let them die without baptism. For this his "better", what word hath he in Scripture?'

The entire Confirmation Service is omitted, though a strongly Calvinistic Catechism is included with such additional questions as, 'What is baptism?' The sources of the Catechism are the Second Prayer Book and a Catechism for the use of schoolmasters said to have been drawn up in 1553 by Poynet, Bishop of Rochester.

From Holy Matrimony the ring is excluded. So are all words pertaining thereto. Thus, 'by giving and receiving of a ring' is removed from the Address. The prayer, 'O Eternal God,' associated with the blessing of the ring, is expunged.

The words, 'with my body I thee worship,' disappear. Bitter objection to this use of the word 'worship' was to be voiced by the Puritans at Hampton Court and the Savoy, as though it implied adoration. There is no provision for Holy Communion.

The Visitation of the Sick remains the same as in the Second Book. But abbreviations are permitted at the discretion of the pastor. The form for the Communion of the Sick is omitted.

The order for Burial remains as in the Second Book.

The Thanksgiving of Women after Childbirth, disliked by Knox, is not included.

CHAPTER II

THE PURITANS

IT is the nature of reformers to be impatient of delay and compromise, and to underrate the immense inertia and conservative instincts of mankind.

The Puritan exiles who returned to England with the accession of Elizabeth were eager to continue the work of Reformation so rudely interrupted by the death of Edward VI. They were soon to discover, to their great chagrin, that the new Geneva, like the old Rome, was not to be built in a day.

The new Queen was a Protestant as much by necessity as conviction. During her sister's reign she had conformed to the old religion. Imperious as her father before her, she had no desire to yield her ecclesiastical supremacy to the pope. Nor did she relish the imputation of bastardy and usurpation, born of the refusal of Clement VII to sanction the marriage of her mother, Anne Boleyn. Elizabeth could scarcely be a Roman Catholic. But her Protestantism was lukewarm. She realised that the majority of her subjects still had leanings towards the old faith, though few wanted the pope, and many preferred a service in English. Neither the crude gangster politics of the Protestant Northumberland, nor the fanatical persecutions of the Catholic Mary had appealed to the nation. Then, as now, the English distrusted extremes of conduct, and had little confidence in logic.

There can be no doubt that many of her subjects shared with Elizabeth a sentimental attachment to the old ways. The Queen was inordinately fond of pageantry, and much approved of the high state that Archbishop Whitgift, 'her little black husband' as she called him, restored to his office. Elizabeth approved of episcopacy, and had no liking for the democratic republicanism of the Church of Geneva. Nor did she wish to lose the countenance of the powerful Catholic princes of the

Continent, upon whose friendship, more politic than genuine, the security of her throne to no small degree depended.

The Elizabethan settlement was fashioned from these circumstances. The Church of England became Protestant, but retained continuity with the ancient *Ecclesia Anglicana*. The papacy, the monasteries, and the Mass were set aside. But the historic episcopate remained. Finally, a Book of Common Prayer was adopted which retained not only Catholic rites but doctrine.

The Puritans were quick to resent a policy that had some appearance of treason to the Reformation. No doubt many shades of opinion were to be found among them. But all had a common loyalty to the Bible, a common hatred of Rome, and a common conviction that nothing should find a place in a prayer book not authorised by the Scriptures. Some, indeed, were of the opinion that the Prayer Book would be better out of the way. Their preference was for some godly liturgy such as the Book of Geneva. But the majority would have been happy enough to accept a Prayer Book purged of Romanism. Such were the opinions of an influential and prosperous group in the community, comprising many members of the rising middle class, the seafaring folk, and the squirearchy.

Elizabeth regarded her policy as a revival of her father's, but the age of the Counter-Reformation required a sterner Protestantism. The Act of Uniformity of 1559 restored, with modifications, not the First but the Second Prayer Book of Edward VI. As such it increasingly won the affections of the nation as a whole. It could not, however, be acceptable to extreme Catholics and Calvinists whose principles forbade adherence to a *via media* compromise.

The extreme Calvinists hoped much from the new reign. The fourth edition of the Book of Geneva (1560) speaks fervently of God's favour, 'in that He hath given us a most virtuous queen, such one as is most desirous herself to set forth God's glory in all her dominions, and most earnestly requireth of all her subjects that with all diligence they embrace the same'. They were speedily disillusioned. The Act of Uniformity put upon the clergy the duty of conducting public worship in strict accord with the Prayer Book, and made it compulsory for all to attend their parish church on Sunday.

It would be wrong to assume that uniformity of worship was attained by the Act of Uniformity. Many clergymen honoured the Act more in the breach than the observance. Nor was it easy for the government to take action. The England of Elizabeth was not a modern totalitarian state. There was no regular army or police force, and the local administrators of government, the justices of the peace, allowed themselves much latitude in their remote country districts. Many of these justices had Puritan sympathies. For some years the greatest disorder prevailed in the Church of England. Sometimes the Prayer Book was strictly observed, sometimes the psalms in metre were added. Sometimes the communion table stood in the middle of the chancel, sometimes altar-wise near the wall. At the celebration of the Holy Communion, some clergymen officiated in a surplice, others recoiled from the 'livery of Antichrist'. Sometimes a chalice was used, sometimes a common cup. Sometimes unleavened bread was taken, sometimes leavened. Some clergymen baptized in a font, others in a basin. Some made the sign of the cross, others thought it one of the 'dregs of popery'. In 1566, Archbishop Parker in his *Book of Advertisements* sought to enforce uniformity by prescribing fixed rules for the conduct of public worship. A number of ministers who refused to submit were deprived. Many more yielded a contemptuous compliance. They were to give a dangerous direction to the attack on the Elizabethan settlement by challenging the whole hierarchical organisation of the Church. Their demand was for the equality of the ministry. 'Bishops must be unlorded.'

The Church of England as established under Elizabeth was a national Church held to be in legitimate and faithful descent from the Undivided Church. As such it was the English branch of the Holy Catholic Church freed from the superstitious errors and accretions of the Middle Ages. But, increasingly, the Puritans challenged this appeal to historical precedent. Under the tutelage of Thomas Cartwright, Lady Margaret Professor of Divinity at Cambridge, they sought for a return to the apostolic age and an ecclesiastical polity based upon the Scriptures. Cartwright demanded a root and branch abolition of 'unscriptural' diocesan episcopacy. He advocated a return to the primitive church, the removal of archbishops and archdeacons, the substitution of presbyteries, and the restoration of bishops to their true apostolic functions of preaching and teaching. This attempt to introduce Calvinistic discipline met with the resistance of John Whitgift. As Master of Trinity College he deprived Cartwright of his fellowship: as Vice-Chancellor of Cambridge University he deprived him of his chair. But Whitgift was to discover that ideas are not so easily liquidated. Cartwright fled abroad in 1574, but by this time Presbyterianism had become the militant creed of very many Puritans. Their attitude was set forth in the Admonition to Parliament of 1571, and in the Second Admonition of 1572. Two years later Cartwright's translation of Walter Travers's *Ecclesiasticae Disciplinae . . . Explicatio* appeared. This was to become the canonical book of Presbyterian nonconformity.

The Elizabethan settlement was based upon Parliamentary authority. Increasingly the Puritans came to feel that what Parliament had sanctioned, Parliament could change. This attitude became the more important as the House of Commons became more Puritan. In 1571 a Bill to reform the Prayer Book was introduced into the Commons by Walter Strickland. But the Queen considered the meddling of the Commons with the Church an outrageous infringement of her prerogative. The Tudor Parliaments were not strong enough to resist the Crown, and the Puritans sought other means to give expression to their views.

Increasingly they promoted 'prophesyings'. These meetings for the study of the Scriptures and the improvement of morals soon became popular, especially in the south-eastern dioceses. The clergy were stimulated to greater zeal and study by the 'exercises', and the laity, who were invited to attend as hearers, were suitably edified. But religious discussion and debate may lead to dangerous attacks on authority. Elizabeth took alarm, and in 1577 gave peremptory orders to her primate Grindal to suppress these meetings, and to discourage preaching. With amazing intrepidity he declined. Thereupon he was suspended from temporal jurisdiction. This was the reprisal lamented by Spenser in his *Shepherd's Calendar*. Grindal is the good Algrind, 'whose hap was ill'.

Edmund Grindal was renowned for his Puritan sympathies. A Royal Chaplain under Edward VI, he had fled to Strasbourg in Mary's reign. At this time the troubles at Frankfort were beginning. Grindal and the Strasbourg divines were shocked by the religious radicalism of their Frankfort brethren. These revolutionaries had abolished the surplice, the Litany, and the versicles. Their service consisted of Scripture sentence and ex- hortation, a Calvinistic confession of sins, not taken from the Prayer Book, but adapted from the Hagenau Missal, a metrical psalm, the minister's prayer for the assistance of God's Holy Spirit, followed by Scripture readings and the sermon, a general prayer for all estates, particularly for England, with the Lord's Prayer, the Apostles' Creed, psalm, and the blessing from the Prayer Book Communion. The Frankfort congregation com- mended this order to the Strasbourg congregation as being more agreeable to Scripture order than King Edward's book. The Zurich divines protested.

The Strasbourg theologians were far from satisfied. Grindal went to Frankfort to urge them to preserve the 'substance and effect' of the Prayer Book. It was pointed out that this book was already sealed with the blood of the martyrs, and that deviation from its use would lay the exiles open to a charge of inconsis- tency. To this reply was made that the martyrs were not dying in defence of ceremonies. But Bishop Ridley, writing to Grindal from his English prison, exclaimed, 'Alas! that our Brother Knox could not bear with our Book of Common Prayer.' Grindal's attempts to compose these differences were un- availing.

The accession of Elizabeth brought him back to England and high honour. He was made one of the commissioners for the revision of the liturgy, and succeeded Bonner as Bishop of London. His position was now most difficult. He was not an extremist. But he had the Puritan's objection to the surplice, and the Puritan's fervour for the Word. As such he could not conscientiously carry out the policy expected of him by Eliza- beth and her Primate Parker. In 1570 the Archbishop of Canterbury was relieved of an embarrassment by Grindal's translation to York. In the northern province the kindly prelate won golden opinions for sincerity and tact. His work was congenial. There was much Roman Catholicism to root out.

The subsequent appointment of Grindal to the See of Canter- bury is one of the astonishing acts of this reign. Only the extraordinary convolutions of Elizabethan politics will account for it. It so happened that in 1575 foreign affairs made some concession to the Puritans advisable. The Queen's minister Cecil was of the opinion that the time had come to attempt a real reconciliation with the Puritans, and that the Archbishop of York was the man to do it. It was Grindal's misfortune that his accession to the primacy of all England was followed by a new approach of Elizabeth to the Catholic princes of the Continent. Hence his brief tenure of power. His dignified protest against the royal interference in Church affairs brought suspension in 1577. Full restoration to authority did not come till the end of 1582. Next year he died. But his influence on the religious life of the nation was considerable. For it was during his primacy that the Geneva Bible came to be printed in England in 1576.

The Geneva Bible, sometimes called the Breeches Bible, had been published by the Genevan exiles in 1560. It was in the main the work of William Whittingham, assisted by Thomas Sampson and Anthony Gilby. Whittingham had been Knox's chief supporter in his troubles with Cox, and had succeeded him as minister at Geneva. In 1563 he became Dean of Durham. The superiority of the Geneva Bible to the Great Bible, appointed to be read in churches, was obvious. It was a better translation and cheaper. It embodied the latest results of biblical criticism. It was convenient to read, being divided into chapters and verses. It had a finer diction than the Great Bible. But the Geneva Bible did not commend itself to Elizabeth and her hierarchy. This was because of the subversive nature of the highly popular marginal notes. The pope was attacked. In a note on Revelation ix, 2 he was described as 'Antichrist', 'King of Hypocrites', 'Satan's ambassador', and more simply elsewhere as 'the villain'. The episcopate was not spared. The locusts which issued from the smoke of the pit, in the apocalyptic vision, were declared to be 'worldly subtle prelates . . . with Archbishops, bishops'. The equality of the clergy was proclaimed in the heading of a page, 'St. Luke, Chapter XXII, 26. God's Ministers Equal'. One reason which prompted James I to promote the publication of his authorised bible was his dislike of the politics preached on the margins of the Geneva Bible. For the notes did not spare kings. Elizabeth's first primate Matthew Parker did his best to meet the challenge of this new Bible, and under his direction the Bishops' Bible was published in 1568. This version was never popular, although it continued to be the official Bible of the Church of England till 1611. Parker successfully withstood any attempt to publish the Geneva Bible in England. But Grindal offered no opposition, and it was printed by Christopher Barker, *cum privilegio*. The Geneva Bible became a great favourite. Between 1560 and 1640 no less than 150 editions were published. Scotsmen loved it. It was the Bible of their reformed church. Shakespeare and most Elizabethan Englishmen read this version. Even after 1611 it remained the Bible of Puritan households.

It was not uncommon for editions of the Bishops' Bible to be combined with the Book of Common Prayer. In 1578 a Geneva Bible was published with a revised edition of the Prayer Book. Other revisions followed. The issue of these Puritan editions has given rise to problems. In his *History of the Book of Common Prayer* (pp. 61-2) Thomas Lathbury writes, the Puritans 'endeavoured to introduce changes into some editions of the Book. A bold, though silent, attempt of this kind was made in 1578. In that year an edition of the Geneva Bible was published in a large folio volume, and to this book was appended a new impression of the Book of Common Prayer, beautifully printed. The Bible was intended by the Puritans to be used in churches instead of the Bishops' Bible of 1568, which had been introduced by royal authority; and as the Book of Common Prayer, in large type, was prefixed to the volume, it was imagined that the clergy might in their ministrations make use of this edition. Still it did not attract much attention at the time. This is evident from Heylyn who, though he mentions a book with the peculiarities of this volume, yet had never seen a copy. The design is apparent from its contents; and the Puritans imagined that a silent and gradual change might be accomplished. Some entire services are altogether omitted, as the office for Private Baptism, that for Confirmation, and that for the Churching of Women. These services were especially obnoxious to the Puritans, and from their Book they are excluded. The first four rubrics in the Communion Service and the introductory rubric in the office for Public Baptism are omitted; and the word "priest" does not occur once in the whole Book.'

Descriptions of the 'Puritan Prayer Book of 1578' are given by W. K. Clay in *Elizabethan Liturgical Services* (1847), and by Proctor and Frere in their *History of the Book of Common Prayer*. More recently Mr. J. F. Gerrard in his *Notable Editions of the Prayer Book* has referred to these Puritan editions. He points out that many show signs of haste in printing, and that variations in the text may be ascribed to the vagaries of early printers. This would account for the alternations of 'priest' with 'minister'. The abridgement of services could be due to an understandable desire to shorten an omnibus volume containing bible, prayer book and perhaps concordances and psalters. Mr. Gerrard does not regard Clay's evidence as conclusive that the Puritans deliberately tampered with the official printing of the statutory text.

But with due respect for this caution, the evidence for a deliberate attempt to introduce a revised Prayer Book is very strong. It is impossible to state with complete certainty that the Puritans intended of set purpose to substitute a revised liturgy for the authorised book. But it is well known they did not hesitate to substitute the Geneva Bible for the authorised Bishops' Bible, and it is difficult to believe they would be more scrupulous about the liturgy.

It is interesting to note that the Geneva Bibles with revised prayer books have two psalters in parallel columns, 'The translation according to the Ebrewe' and 'The translation used in Common Prayer', as in the folio edition of the Bishops' Bible of 1572. The Common Prayer translation is divided into portions for Morning and Evening Prayer. This looks like a provision for Public Service. Puritan revisions no doubt display the usual aberrations of Tudor printers. But it is remarkable that none of these revisions is identical with the authorised liturgy. Many of the Geneva Bibles with prayer books are large and impressive tomes. It is difficult to see the advantage of economy of space in volumes of this size.

Nor does the nature of the omissions accord with Mr. Gerrard's suggestion that the editors intended to produce a 'portable library of Divinity'. Obvious omissions would have been the proper lessons and proper psalms, the almanack, and the calendar with the table of lessons for every day of the year. But these are included in the 1578 edition and were frequently reprinted. Other omissions have theological implications. Thus the 1578 Prayer Book deletes the introductory rubrics to the Communion Service, but the very lengthy final rubrics are retained.

Moreover, the authority of Peter Heylyn may not be lightly dismissed. This distinguished divine was chaplain to Charles I and Charles II. Born in 1600, he was acquainted intimately with the vexed ecclesiastical problems of Tudors and Stuarts. In his *History of the Presbyterians*, called by him *Aerius Redivivus*, he comments with some asperity on the friendship maintained by Grindal with Calvin, Beza, Zanchy and others of the school of Geneva, even after his accession to the episcopate. 'Under these grounds the Presbyterians gave themselves good hopes of the new Archbishop', when Grindal was translated to Canterbury in 1575. Then come the references to the Puritan Prayer Book. 'They ventured on a business of a higher nature, which was the falsifying and corrupting of the Common Prayer Book. In which, being then published by Richard Jugge, the Queen's Majesty's Printer, and published *Cum Privilegio Regiae Magestatis*, as the title intimates, the whole order of Private Baptism and Confirmation of Children was quite omitted. In the first of it it had been declared, "That children being born in original sin, were by the laver of regeneration in baptism ascribed unto the number of God's Children, and made the heirs of life eternal", and in the other, "That by the imposition of hands and prayer, they received strength against sin, the world, and the devil". Which grand omissions were designed to no other purpose, but by degrees to bring the Church of England into some conformity to the desired orders of Geneva. This I find noted in the preface of a book writ by William Reynolds, a virulent papist I confess, but one that may be credited in a matter of fact, which might so easily have been refuted by the Book itself, if he had any way belied it' (*Aerius Redivivus*, Second Edition 1672, p. 245). Heylyn concludes with the comment that nothing was done 'for punishing of this great abuse'.

But the most important reason for believing that the Puritan editors of these liturgies were not innocent of a design to modify the Prayer Book is derived from their known hostility to parts of the services, and their constant attempts to remove them.

This had been apparent at Frankfort. It was in evidence again, in the years following 1572, when the Puritans deliberately altered the Prayer Book. This was one of the features of their 'classical movement'. The basis of the scheme was the introduction of a Presbyterian discipline into Episcopacy. The 'classis' was a secret synod composed of all the clergy in a diocese willing to subscribe to Travers's book of discipline. The object was to adapt the Anglican polity to the Presbyterian, while keeping within the law. Congregations were to elect their ministers, and to recommend them through the 'classis' to the bishop for ordination. Puritan interpretations of the Scriptures were to be used in preaching, and offending passages in the Prayer Book left out. Records of the Dedham Conference show how frequently the Puritan members debated between the years 1582–9, 'how far a pastor might go in reading the Book of Common Prayer'. Furthermore, the petition of the House of Commons for ecclesiastical reform in 1584 makes a special plea that 'such ministers as in the public service of the Church and the administration of the sacraments do use the Book of Common Prayer allowed in the statutes of this realm, and none other, be not from henceforth called in question for omissions or changes of some portions or rite.' It is not surprising if at such a time the insertion of Puritan Prayer Books in Geneva Bibles was attempted.

Revised prayer books continued to be printed with the large Geneva Bible very regularly until 1616. After this time the superlative merits of the Authorised Version won increasing favour. Small Geneva Bibles with Puritan variations continued to be published till 1640, and were in use till long after. In the London Bible House is a tiny edition of a Jacobean Puritan liturgy, bound up with a Genevan version of the New Testament. Prayers are included for King James, Queen Anne, Prince Charles and the Elector Palatine. A list of solemn days has been added for which particular services are appointed. They include 29th May, the Restoration Day of Charles II in 1660.

The audacity of the Puritans in printing revisions, and the curious willingness of the government to permit their publication by the same individuals who enjoyed the monopoly of printing the Authorised Prayer Book have caused historians some astonishment (*Elizabethan Liturgical Services*, W. K. Clay, Introduction, p. xviii). But the very nature of the revisions must have facilitated their issue. To all outward appearance they were abridgements only. There was no obvious rearrangement or alteration of the Prayer Book, such as distinguished the Deposited Book of 1928. There was no heretical doctrine introduced as with the Semi-Arian revisions of the eighteenth century. The Puritans desired a liturgy purged of Romanism, but they had no basic doctrinal quarrel with the episcopate. Bishops and Puritans alike at this period were Calvinists. In 1578 Calvin's Catechism was approved by the University of Oxford. In 1595 Archbishop Whitgift's nine 'Lambeth Articles' adopted Calvinist views of predestination and election.

But there is a further reason why the Puritan revisions escaped censure. Historians have noted in detail the first Puritan edition of 1578. They have commented also on the much closer approximations to the authorised book of later editions. Writing of the 1578 book, Procter and Frere say: 'It seems that this was too bold an experiment; or the party could not agree in any uniform practice.' They point out that in 1589 a revision is found with the services for Private Baptism and the Churching of Women restored. In actual fact this change was made much earlier. In 1579 two editions of the Puritan revision were published. One was an exact reproduction of 1578, the other was the 1578 book with the addition of services for Private Baptism, Confirmation, and the Churching of Women. It was this revision which tended to be reprinted, and its clever and specious likeness to the authorised liturgy must have made detection the more difficult. Puritan revisions were discreet. Thus no attempt was made to restore to the Litany a clause dear to the heart of Puritans, 'from the tyranny of the Bishop of Rome and all his detestable enormities . . . Good Lord, deliver us'. The use of the cross was enjoined in Public Baptism, and the ring in Marriage. Communicants were required to kneel for the reception of the elements in Holy Communion, and absolution was retained in this service and the order for the Visitation of the Sick. Collects for Saints' Days remained.

It must be remembered that subsequent amendments of the Prayer Book have tended to make the authorised liturgy of today more Catholic in character than was Elizabeth's book.

Thus the Puritan revisions could not have been so noticeable then as now. The frequent use of the word 'congregation' instead of 'church' is a feature of Elizabeth's book. King James himself ordered the translators of the Authorised Version of the Bible not to use 'congregation' for 'church'. Also, in the Elizabethan Litany the words 'Bishops, Pastors, and Ministers of the Church' occur in the place where the Litany of today reads, 'Bishops, Priests, and Deacons'.

Finally, it is to be remembered that the assumption sometimes made that the Puritans were a persecuted minority during the whole of Elizabeth's reign is incorrect. Until the defeat of the Armada in 1588, they enjoyed a remarkable freedom from governmental interference. This was due to the civil authorities' preoccupation with the far greater menace of Roman Catholicism. The Northern Rebellion of 1569, the Papal Bull of excommunication and deposition of Elizabeth in 1570, and the Jesuit mission of Parsons and Campion in 1580 kept the Queen's Council in a constant state of alarm. More sinister was the might of Philip II of Spain and the disturbing presence of the Catholic Queen of Scots in her State prison. The Puritans were zealous anti-Romanists. Such enthusiasts were too useful to suppress.

One singular feature of the Puritan Prayer Book is the extraordinary divergence of Tudor and Jacobean editions. Prayer Books published by Puritans after 1603 are much closer approximations to the authorised Book of Common Prayer. Indeed, a few editions are almost identical with the legitimate book. One such edition is the 1607 Puritan Prayer Book in the London Bible House. It contains the King's Proclamation 'for the authorising and uniformity of the book of common prayer to be used throughout the realm'. This proclamation, issued in the first year of the reign of James I, reads: 'We do admonish all men, that hereafter they shall not expect nor attempt any further alteration in the Common Public form of God's service, from this which is now established, for that neither will we give way to any to presume, that our own judgement having determined in a matter of this weight, shall be swayed to alteration by the frivolous suggestions of any light spirit.'

The fact is that towards the end of Elizabeth's reign, the Puritans were finding their position much more precarious.

The defeat of the Spanish Armada in 1588 had released the government from an overriding fear of Rome. It was unfortunate for the Puritans that in the same year they lost by death their outstanding champion at Court, the Earl of Leicester. Nor had their cause been served by the violence of the Martin Marprelate attack on the bishops. The English do not like violence. The weakened state of the Puritans gave an opportunity to their most redoubtable adversary. Richard Bancroft appeared on the high commission in 1587. In 1597 he became Bishop of London, and in 1604 Archbishop of Canterbury. The temper of the times can be seen by the drastic Conventicle Act of 1593 which decreed exile or a felon's death for those obstinately refusing to attend the parish church.

The long reign of Elizabeth had strengthened her religious settlement, and a generation was growing up with a love for her Church of England. The publication of Richard Hooker's *Ecclesiastical Polity* in 1594 provided episcopacy with a judicious and majestic defence.

Under these circumstances, the Puritans, a religious minority, consisting of groups which were by no means united, found themselves in a serious plight. This is reflected in the increasing caution of their liturgical revisions.

HOW THE PURITAN PRAYER BOOKS WERE REVISED

The Puritan revision of 1578 was followed by an identical edition in 1579. The following changes are made. In the Table of Proper Lessons, 'For Morning' and 'For Evening' are substituted for 'Mattins' and 'Evensong'. The word 'priest' is replaced by 'minister' throughout the revision, save in the Benedicite. In the Communion Service, the introductory rubrics are omitted, and 'great number' substituted for 'good number' in the second rubric at the end. In the ministration of Public Baptism, the introductory rubric with the words, 'children may at all times be baptized at home' is deleted, and the charge that children be brought to the bishop for confirmation omitted. Private Baptism and Confirmation are expunged. Only the third rubric is retained in the Communion of the Sick. Churching is not included.

In 1579 a new revision was published. At least twelve other

editions of this revision were issued during the remainder of Elizabeth's reign. The 1579 revision is a replica of the 1578 revision, apart from the following additional changes. The charge that children be brought to the bishop for confirmation is restored. Private Baptism and Churching are reinserted, with the word 'priest' significantly reintroduced. 'Great number' is replaced by 'good number' in the second rubric at the end of the Communion Service, in the 1592 and subsequent editions.

A new Puritan revision was published in 1603 and at least eight other editions were published up to 1616. The 1603 revision is a replica of the 1579 revision, with still further changes. Thus the introductory rubrics and the word 'priest' are restored to the Communion Service. In Public Baptism the introductory rubric is reinserted. Confirmation is included once more, and the word 'priest' brought back to the Communion of the Sick.

One further revision is to be observed. This is a Puritan approximation to the authorised Book of Common Prayer. Editions appeared in 1592, 1607 and 1613 (?). In the Table of Proper Lessons, the words 'Mattins' and 'Evensong' reappear. The word 'priest' is restored to the versicles in Morning and Evening Prayer, and to its place in the Communion Service. All occasional services are retained, and the word 'priest' nowhere deleted. Changes in Elizabethan and Jacobean revisions are indicated in the table on pages 33–4.

WHY THE PURITAN PRAYER BOOKS WERE REVISED

The Puritans disliked the name 'Mattins'. This was because it denoted in the Roman Church one of the 'hours' or daily services of the breviary. Hence their preference for 'Morning Prayer.' Similarly the word 'Evensong' was suspect through association with 'Vespers', another of the Roman canonical Hours of Prayer. The revisers preferred 'Evening Prayer'.

The Puritans objected to the word 'priest' because of the attendant idea of sacrifice. Thus the priests of the line of Aaron were sacrificing priests, and the Roman Catholic clergy daily offered the sacrifice of the Mass. The Puritans held that the sacrifice of Calvary was all-sufficient, and that the Lord Jesus was the one great sacrificing High Priest for ever. They sought, therefore, to substitute 'minister' for 'priest', and later made a proposal to this effect at the Savoy Conference. The word 'priest' was changed to 'minister' in the 1578 revision, except in the Benedicite, 'O Ye Priests of the Lord, bless ye the Lord'. This solitary exception does not appear to have been noticed by Lathbury or by Procter and Frere. But its inclusion is significant. The Puritans disapproved of the Benedicite as apocryphal. The odious word was included in the odious canticle. It is almost certain that 'priest' was intended to be a word of warning to the faithful. This became apparent with the publication of the 1579 revision. The obnoxious services of Private Baptism and Churching were restored, but the obnoxious 'priest' reappeared. It seems that Clay was right when he suggested that this was 'a silent, but intelligible sign that the use of the services themselves was meant to be discouraged' (Preface, p. xvii). At first it would seem that the variations of 'priest' and 'minister' in the Puritan revisions are bewildering, if not chaotic. In fact they are illuminating. Apart from the Benedicite, the word 'priest' was expunged ruthlessly from Morning and Evening Prayer, the services the Puritans habitually used. In the occasional services two methods were employed. The first was to substitute 'minister' for 'priest', thus striking at the concept of sacerdotalism. The other was to employ the word 'priest' in those services the Puritans wished to see deleted from the Prayer Book.

The revisers omitted the introductory rubrics to the Communion Service. But they regularized their position by referring the reader for them to the 'Great Book of Common Prayer'. This was a somewhat equivocal device. The omission could be justified as an abridgement. But for reasons already stated this explanation is not very probable. The very lengthy rubrics at the end of the office were not removed. The following direction was expunged: 'if any of those be an open and notorious evil liver . . . the Curate, having knowledge thereof, shall call him and advertise him, that in any wise he presume not to come to the Lord's Table, until he hath openly declared himself to have truly repented and amended his former naughty life. . . .' The fact was that the Puritans of this period were incensed with the abuses of excommunication. In 1584 the House of Commons sent a petition to the House of Lords. It contained this plea:

'Where complaint is made of the abuse of excommunication
. . . it may please your lordships to consider whether some bill
might not be conveniently framed to this effect, viz: That none
having ecclesiastical jurisdiction shall in any matter . . . other
than in the cases hereafter mentioned, give or pronounce any
sentence of excommunication. . . . Nevertheless, forasmuch as
it seemeth not meet that the Church should be left without this
censure of excommunication, it may be provided that for
enormous crimes, as incest, adultery and such like, the same be
executed by the reverend fathers the bishops themselves with
the assistance of grave persons.' Next year, a Puritan petition
was presented to the Queen. It advocated the associating of
laymen with the bishops and clergy for the hearing of 'every
cause ecclesiastical'. Furthermore, it sought that 'no one bishop
do hereafter proceed in excommunicating any faulty person,
nor in absolving any person that is excommunicated, without
the advice and consent of the aforesaid seniors and associates
joined with him'. It is to be remembered that, although
Presbyterians considered it the duty of the minister to warn
against irreverent participation in Communion, exclusion from
the Sacrament depended on the decision of minister and elders
in session.

The Puritan revisers removed the rubric permitting the
communion table to 'stand in the body of the Church, or in
the chancel'. The reason for this omission is more difficult to
find since the Puritans cannot have objected to the Holy Table
being 'in the body of the Church'. It may be that they did not
regard this rubric as a very serious concession. In Elizabethan
times 'God's board' was moved around in a free and easy
fashion, and great was 'the ferment among the common people'
when Laud and his reforming bishops ordered the Table to
remain at the east end of the Chancel. It was not uncommon at
this period for communicants to receive the elements in their
pews. This practice long survived, notably at Oxford when
Newman was vicar of St. Mary's. Nor is it unlikely that some
Tudor Puritans saw in the rubric more than a suspicion of the
hated altar. The priest is directed to stand at the 'North-
side of the Table'. But Scudamore, in his *Notitia Eucharistica*,
observes that some were of opinion that the North-side had
been chosen as that side of the Jewish altar where sacrificial

victims were wont to be slain. The Puritans were Old Testament readers. They cannot have been ignorant of Leviticus, i, 10, 11, 'And if his offering be of the flocks, namely, of the sheep, or of the goats, for a burnt sacrifice; he shall bring it a male without blemish. And he shall kill it on the side of the altar northward before the Lord: and the priests, Aaron's sons, shall sprinkle his blood round about upon the altar.' The Jewish priest of the Tabernacle stood on the liturgical north side when offering sacrifice. The Puritan objection to the sacrificing priest is well known.

The Puritan editors substituted 'great number' for 'good number' in the second rubric at the end of the Communion Service. They wished to avoid any possibility of private celebrations of the Sacraments. Puritans remembered with horror the Mass priest and the chantry. This is the reason why the third rubric only was retained in the Communion of the Sick.

Antipathy to private celebrations was responsible for the omission of the introductory rubric in Public Baptism. The words, 'Children may at all times be baptized at home' countenanced Private Baptism, obnoxious to the Puritans as a private celebration sanctioned by the Roman Catholic Church.

The Puritans disliked Confirmation. They considered that it was unwise for children to be confirmed as soon as they could repeat the Lord's Prayer and the Catechism. Such a practice could lead to children of very tender age receiving Communion, without any consideration of spiritual fitness. They believed that there was danger in the bishop's laying on of hands, as this might seem to imply some special sacramental efficacy.

The Puritans disliked the Churching of Women as much too like the Jewish purification. Knox and his friends in their letter to Calvin made objection to it since it 'is not only in all things almost common with the Papists, but also with the Jews, because they are commended instead of a lamb or dove to offer money' (*Trouble at Frankfort*, p. xxxiii).

PURITAN REVISIONS OF THE PRAYER BOOK

TABLE SHOWING PROCESS OF CHANGE

B.M. = British Museum.
B.H. = Bible House, London.
BOD. = Bodleian Library, Oxford.
J.R. = John Rylands Library, Manchester.

I. PURITAN PRAYER BOOK OF 1578

Table of Proper Lessons. 'For Morning' and 'For Evening' substituted
for 'Mattins' and 'Evensong'.
'Minister' is substituted for 'Priest' (except in the Benedicite).
Communion. Introductory rubrics omitted.
'Great number' substituted for 'good number' in second
rubric at end of service.
Public Baptism. Introductory rubric with words, 'children may at all
times be baptized at home' omitted. Charge that children be
brought to the bishop for confirmation omitted.
Private Baptism. Omitted.
Confirmation. Omitted.
Communion of the Sick. Third rubric only retained.
Churching. Omitted.

Edition	Library
1578	J.R.
1579	B.H.

II. THE NEW PURITAN PRAYER BOOK OF 1579

The new 1579 Puritan Prayer Book is an archetype.
It is a replica of the Puritan Prayer Book of 1578, but for the
following changes.
Public Baptism. Charge that children be brought to the bishop for
confirmation restored.
Private Baptism. Restored, with the word 'priest'.
Churching. Restored, with the word 'priest'.
N.B. Editions of 1592 and afterwards replace 'great number' by
'good number' in second rubric at end of Communion Service.

Edition	Library
1579	B.H.
1580	B.H.
1580	B.H.
1581	B.H.
1582	BOD.
1583	B.M.
1585	B.H.

33

1589	Reference by Procter and Frere	
1592		B.H.
1594 (?)	Incorporated with 1598 Geneva Bible	J.R.
1596		B.H.
1597		BOD.
1597		B.M.

III. JACOBEAN REVISIONS OF THE PURITAN PRAYER BOOK

This group of Puritan Prayer Books, published in the reign of James I, is the archetype of 1579, but for still further changes.
Communion. Introductory rubrics restored.
        The word 'priest' restored.
Public Baptism. Introductory rubric restored.
Confirmation. Restored.
Communion of the Sick. The word 'priest' restored.
        Rubric restored.

Edition		*Library*
1603		B.H.
1606		B.H.
1607		J.R.
1608		J.R.
1611	Incorporated with 1612 Geneva Bible	B.H.
1614		B.H.
1614	Incorporated with 1615 Geneva Bible	B.H.
1615		B.H.
1616		B.H.

IV. PURITAN APPROXIMATIONS TO AUTHORISED PRAYER BOOK

This last group is a Puritan approximation to the authorised Book of Common Prayer.

It embodies the changes of the previous groups with the following additions.

Table of Proper Lessons. The words 'Mattins' and 'Evensong' are restored.

'Priest' is restored to the versicles in Morning and Evening Prayer, and to the Communion service. Nowhere is it deleted in the occasional services.

Occasional Services. All are included.

Edition		*Library*
1592	Very incomplete. Communion office not included	J.R.
1607	Incorporated with 1610 Geneva Bible	B.H.
1613 (?)	Authorised B.C.P. with Genevan New Testament	B.H.

CHAPTER III

THE METHODISTS

JOHN WESLEY was the son of a High Church rector of Epworth. He was also, as Mrs. Harrison reminds us in a delightful book, *Son to Susanna*. From this early environment the Founder of Methodism never escaped. He remained to the end of his days very much a High Churchman of the old school. But the sensitive conscience of the young Wesley was quickened by the piety of his mother. Susanna was not for nothing the daughter of a great Puritan divine. On the night when her little son was rescued from their blazing homestead, the mother saw in him a brand plucked from the burning. Henceforth she resolved to be 'particularly careful of his soul'. Solicitude for his soul, and for the souls of others, was to become the passion of his life. It made him, when a young Fellow of Lincoln, leader of the 'Holy Club'. Significantly, the piety of the Holy Club was fostered by the Prayer Book. In Georgia, John Wesley showed himself a true son of his father in his antagonism to Dissenters. The colonists were amazed to see how punctilious was this clergyman on such points of primitive usage as the immersion of infants at baptism, and the use of the mixed chalice. The first Methodist laid more than a little emphasis on the invocation and prothesis in the Sacrament of the Altar, prayers for the faithful departed, the Stations of the Cross, and the Eastward position for the Creed. His critics in Georgia made angry comment: 'We are Protestants'. It is all the more remarkable, therefore, that it was the voyage to Georgia that was the means of introducing him to a new influence. One Sunday there was storm at sea. Fear swept the deck, save among some Moravian emigrants. John marvelled at their courage. His tender heart was moved at their strange, wistful hymns that spoke of God as though in some love song. On

35

his return to England, Wesley met the Moravian leader Peter Boehler. Through him he was led into spiritual rest. The first step was the conviction of want of faith. On 24th May 1738, Wesley attended a religious society in Aldersgate Street, London. There he heard a member read Luther's 'Preface to the Epistle to the Romans'. 'About a quarter before nine, while he was describing the change which God works in the heart through faith in Christ, I felt my heart strangely warmed. I felt I did trust in Christ, Christ alone, for salvation.' It is impossible to exaggerate the importance of this conversion. Lecky maintains that it marks 'an epoch in English history'. It does more, for Methodism is now the largest Church of the English-speaking race. But although the conversion of Wesley is the *fons et origo* of Methodism, it would be a mistake to assume that the Evangelical in him completely absorbed the High Churchman. Wesley broke with the Moravians because all his old instincts revolted against their mystical tendency to despise the external duties of religion. To the end of his days there was, as Professor Peake has said, 'a double strain within him, the conservative and the revolutionary'.

It was the revolutionary strain that mattered most. It was the joy of being free at last from the burden of unpardoned sin that made him preach his gospel to a world that was his parish. 'I felt I did trust in Christ, Christ alone for salvation; and an assurance was given me that He had taken away my sins, even mine, and saved me from the law of sin and death.' The doctrine of assurance, a personal certainty of forgiveness and of restored sonship to God, was the outstanding feature of original Methodism. This doctrine was associated with 'the second blessing' or sanctification. This postulated that it was not impossible for an experience of pardon to be accompanied by complete victory over sin. Wesley believed that the very roots of sin could be extirpated from human nature. His doctrine of universal redemption broke the fetters of predestination. His sermon on 'Free Grace' (1739) released many souls from 'absolute despair'. 'You represent God', he cried to the Calvinists, 'as worse than the devil.' It is not easy for the modern mind to appreciate that Free Grace spelled a deliverance.

Father, whose everlasting love
Thy only Son for sinners gave,
Whose grace to all did freely move,
And sent Him down the world to save:
Thy undistinguishing regard
Was cast on Adam's fallen race;
For all Thou hast in Christ prepared
Sufficient, sovereign, saving grace.

But here again it is necessary to recall the circumstances of Wesley's upbringing. As an adherent of the Laudian theology, Wesley was an Arminian. The High Churchman and the Evangelical were here at one.

It is not necessary to tell again the story of this famous apostleship. For the purposes of this study one fact only need be recalled. As time went on, Wesley found himself compelled to sacrifice his conservative to his revolutionary instincts. Professor Peake has said, 'He took to new paths or followed where others had led the way, crucifying his natural prejudices, adopting irregular means where regular means were not open to him or had been found unavailing.' He preferred the seemly services of the parish church. But when these were closed to him he resorted to field preaching. He had a belief in an ordered ministry and the Apostolical Succession. But he came to countenance lay preachers, at the promptings of the Holy Spirit. Methodists see in his assent to such innovations submission to a guiding Providence. But Charles Wesley was not persuaded. It seemed to him that lay preachers were worse than Nonconformist ministers, and they were bad enough! Writing to John Nelson he exclaimed: 'Rather than see thee a dissenting minister, I wish to see thee smiling in thy coffin.' The founder of Methodism was not to be deterred, though every instinct of his brother was outraged. The conviction came to him that an uninterrupted Apostolical Succession was a fable, and that bishops and presbyters were of the same order. Aware of the crying need of ministers for America he ordained an Anglican clergyman as a 'superintendent' for the New World. It is true he did not countenance Dr. Coke's assumption of the episcopal title, but it was Charles who wrote in scorn:

37

How easily are bishops made
By man or woman's whim!
Wesley his hands on Coke hath laid,
But who laid hands on him?

The compelling motive behind these ordinations was the necessity of meeting the spiritual needs of the New World, which the Church of England had failed to do. For John Wesley spiritual needs were ever paramount. Thus it had been his intention that the members of his societies should attend the services of the parish churches, and particularly the Holy Communion. His preachments were not to take place during church hours. But he was unable to maintain such limitations for his 'preaching houses'. Though not recognizing them as 'churches', he licensed them in accordance with the terms of the Toleration Act. Moreover he made legal provision for their continuance after his death. Even his high doctrine of the sacraments he came to modify. For to the baptized as to the unbaptized the warning would be given: 'Ye must be born again.'

It is easy to understand how Methodism, after the death of the Founder, quickly assumed the character by which it is known today. But just as Wesley never lost all of his High Church leanings, so has Methodism preserved something of them. This is the paradox of Methodism.

Originally, the movement was as much a sacramental as an evangelical revival. Professor Horton Davies has given emphasis to this undoubted fact in a recent volume. The 'combination of a convinced High Churchman's appreciation of liturgy and the Eucharist with a practical if reluctant recognition of the value of extemporary preaching, free prayer, and hymns made Wesley's liturgical contributions the most important single fact in the history of English Christianity in the eighteenth century' (from *Watts and Wesley to Maurice, 1690–1850*). Two centuries later the combination of liturgical and free types of worship survives as a characteristic of Methodism. It has given rise to a Sacramental Fellowship. And the Prayer Book has not been repudiated.

John Wesley's devotion to the Prayer Book never wavered. When late in life he prepared his revision he wrote in the preface: 'I believe there is no Liturgy in the World, either in ancient or modern language, which breathes more of a solid, scriptural, rational piety, than the Common Prayer of the Church of England. And though the main of it was compiled considerably more than two hundred years ago, yet is the language of it, not only pure, but strong and elegant in the highest degree.' As an Anglican clergyman he enjoined Prayer Book worship upon his followers. As a sacramentalist he expounded the high significance of the Communion office. In one of his Standard Sermons he writes of the Eucharist: 'Is not the eating of that bread and the drinking of that cup, the outward visible means whereby God conveys into our souls that spiritual grace, that righteousness and peace and joy in the Holy Ghost which were purchased by the Body of Christ once broken, and the Blood of Christ once shed for us? Let us therefore who truly desire the Grace of God, eat that Bread and drink that Blood.' This language is not surprising when it is recalled that the hymns of Charles Wesley presume the Real Presence. Early in Methodist history it became the first rule of the 'bands' that members should 'be at Church and at the Lord's Table every week'. This is the more remarkable when it is remembered how infrequent were weekly communions at this time. The Anglican clergy were dumbfounded at the number of Methodists who came to communicate. Many were not well received. Some were repelled. The pressure inside the Connexion became insistent that their own preachers should administer. Wesley resisted for long, until at length conviction came that 'soul-damning clergymen laid him under more difficulties than soul-saving laymen'. There was joy among the faithful when they met at last at the Lord's Table in their own congregations. Even so, in Wesley's day, the Eucharist was celebrated only by ordained clergymen of the Church of England. Methodists anticipated the Anglo-Catholics in the revival of frequent communions. But later their observance declined. It has been left to the Sacramental Fellowship to recall Methodists to the example of the Founder. The opinion has been expressed by Dr. J. E. Rattenbury, in his *Vital Elements of Public Worship*, that Holy Communion should take place every Sunday morning as the central act of public worship.

Wesley always considered the Church of England to be the

best constituted national Church in the world. But in the new American Republic there was no national Church. Hence he permitted himself a latitude of action across the Atlantic which he was reluctant to allow himself at home. It was to the New World that he dispatched the first Methodist bishop. Previously he had entreated the Bishop of London to ordain a 'pious man' for America. But his complaisant Lordship had made answer that already there were three ministers in that country! Wesley felt his scruples to be at an end. As 'a Scriptural bishop' he set apart Dr. Coke as superintendent or bishop of a Scriptural and Primitive Church. Moreover, he considered himself free to revise the Prayer Book for a land where the Episcopal Church had been shattered by war. In a letter to 'Dr. Coke, Mr. Asbury, and our Brethren in North America' Wesley justified his action. He explained his right as a presbyter to ordain. He enlarged on the position in America, where 'for hundreds of miles together there is none either to baptize or to administer the Lord's Supper.' He added: 'I have prepared a Liturgy.' This edition was published in 1784. Charles Wesley had cautioned his brother that what was sanctioned for America would have to be countenanced at home. Within two years a new edition of the revision was published for use in England. It was entitled *The Sunday Service of the Methodists with other Occasional Services* (1786).

Not only had Wesley published a book for his followers at home. He had brought forth a revision that was in the true Puritan tradition. That this is so the following evidence is designed to show.

In all places the word 'priest' is changed to 'minister', or, in the Communion, to 'elder'. The Puritans at the Hampton Court Conference had sought for the omission of the word 'priest'. The Presbyterians at the Savoy Conference had asked that the words 'priest' and 'curate' in the Prayer Book should be changed to 'minister'. The Royal Commission of 1689 had been prepared to alter 'priest' to 'minister'.

All Apocryphal lessons are excluded by Wesley. An attempt had been made to meet the wishes of the Puritans in 1604 by the substitution of Old Testament lessons for Bel and the Dragon and Tobit v, 6 and 8. Both the Committee of the House of Lords (1641) and the Presbyterians at the Savoy had objected to all Apocryphal readings. But the 1662 edition restored Bel and the Dragon. The Commission of 1689 had substituted for Apocryphal lessons chapters taken chiefly from Proverbs and Ecclesiastes.

All Saints' Days are expunged by Wesley. The Puritans in 1604 maintained that the observance of Holy Days should be optional. The Presbyterians in 1661 wished to omit them altogether. Knox had regarded them as 'papistical superstition'.

There are no services of Private Baptism, Confirmation, Churching, or Visitation of the Sick in Wesley's revision. There are no general rubrics. This is very much in keeping with Puritan thought. (See Chapter II.)

The other changes are as follows:

MORNING PRAYER

This service is shortened. Wesley remarks in his preface: 'The Service of the Lord's Day, the length of which has been often complained of, is considerably shortened.' Long before, at the Hampton Court Conference, the Puritans had advocated the abridgement of morning services.

EXHORTATION

The Exhortation is removed.

THE ABSOLUTION

The words, 'The Absolution, or Remission of sins', are omitted. This prayer is substituted for the Absolution: 'O Lord, we beseech thee, absolve thy people from their offences; that, through thy bountiful goodness, we may be delivered from the bonds of those sins, which by our frailty we have committed. Grant this, O heavenly Father, for Jesus Christ's sake, our blessed Lord and Saviour.' It will be remembered that the Puritans at the Hampton Court Conference objected to the word Absolution because of its Romish associations.

BENEDICITE

The Benedicite is removed. The Presbyterian divines at the Savoy Conference objected to the Benedicite as Apocryphal.

BENEDICTUS

The Benedictus is removed.

THE SECOND LORD'S PRAYER AND VERSICLES

These are not included. The Presbyterians at the Savoy Conference objected to the too frequent use of the Lord's Prayer. They considered that responses and versicles disturbed the solemnity of prayer, and interrupted the services by vain repetitions.

PRAYER FOR THE KING'S MAJESTY

This prayer omits, 'the only Ruler of princes'.

PRAYER FOR THE CLERGY AND PEOPLE

'Bishops and Curates' are replaced by 'all the Ministers of thy Gospel.'

A PRAYER OF SAINT CHRYSOSTOM

This prayer is retained, without the title.
N.B. In the Prayer for all conditions of men, Wesley retains, 'Catholic Church'.

EVENING PRAYER

The Magnificat is removed. Among the reforms suggested by the Royal Commission of 1689 was the omission of the Magnificat and the Nunc Dimittis. It was maintained by many Prayer Book reformers that they were unsuitable for public worship as referring to particular events and people.

CANTATE DOMINO

This is retained, but the musical instruments are not permitted.

NUNC DIMITTIS

The Nunc Dimittis is removed.

QUICUNQUE VULT

This Creed is omitted. The Presbyterians had disliked the damnatory clause, protesting against the requirement to 'assent and consent to St. Athanasius his creed'.

THE LITANY

The Litany is to be read, not on Sundays, but on Wednesdays and Fridays.

'Bishops, Priests, and Deacons' are changed in the intercession to 'all the Ministers of thy Gospel'. The intercession for the Lords of the Council and the Nobility is omitted. It is interesting to note that the suffrages retain 'sudden death' and 'deadly sin'.

OCCASIONAL PRAYERS AND THANKSGIVING

These are deleted, but the collect for all Conditions of Men, and The General Thanksgiving are included in Morning and Evening Prayer.

COLLECTS, EPISTLES, GOSPELS

These are retained, save for St. Stephen's Day, St. John the Evangelist's Day, the Innocents' Day, the Circumcision of Christ, the Epiphany, the Conversion of Saint Paul, the Purification of Saint Mary, the Annunciation of the Virgin Mary, Saints' Days, and All Saints' Day. No mention is made of Epiphany or Lent. Presbyterians at the Savoy had proposed 'that there be nothing in the Liturgy countenancing the observance of Lent as a Religious Fast'. In the Abridgement 'The Second Sunday after the Epiphany' becomes 'The Third Sunday after Christmas'. Again, 'The Sunday called Septuagesima, or the third Sunday before Lent', becomes 'The Eighth Sunday after Christmas'. 'The First Sunday in Lent', becomes 'The Eleventh Sunday after Christmas'. Collects, Epistles and Gospels for Ash Wednesday and Easter Even are removed. It is to be noted that they are retained for Christmas Day, Good Friday, Easter Day, Ascension Day, Whitsunday and Trinity Sunday. It may be observed, in passing, that the Calendar with the table of lessons for every day of the year is omitted by Wesley. Moreover he commits two liturgical blunders, as Mr. Wesley F. Swift pointed out in an article in *The London Quarterly and Holborn Review* (October, 1958). Wesley ignores Epiphany and Lent, with the result that the Four Sundays of Advent are followed by 'fifteen Sundays after Christmas', which in turn are followed by the Sunday before Easter and then Easter Day; i.e. seventeen Sundays after Christmas up to and including Easter Day. But the Prayer Book makes provision for eighteen such Sundays. Thus, in Wesley's Revision the Prayer Book lessons for the fifth Sunday in Lent disappear! Again, in his revision of the Collects, Epistles and Gospels, he overlooks the fact that the Prayer Book makes no provision in the 'Propers' for the Second Sunday after Christmas as such. The Prayer Book rubric directs that on the second Sunday after Christmas (when it occurs liturgically) the Collect, Epistle and Gospel for the Circumcision of Christ (1st January) are to be read. But Wesley takes no cognizance of this feast, and omits it altogether. The result is that his 'Propers' skip from the First Sunday after Christmas to the First Sunday after Epiphany, which he styles the Second Sunday after Christmas. So Wesley's 'Propers', like his lessons, are one Sunday short of the full required number, though the missing Sundays are not identical.

THE LORD'S SUPPER

There is only one rubric. 'The Table at the Communion-time, having a fair white Linen Cloth upon it, shall stand in some convenient Place. And the Elder, standing at the Table, shall say the Lord's Prayer, with the collect following, the People kneeling.' It will be recalled that the Elizabethan Puritans entertained scruples about the rubrics. It will be noticed that communicants are expected to kneel. Today, this is little observed.

THE NICENE CREED

This is not included, probably so as to shorten the service. It was restored in 1864.

HOLY DAYS, FASTING DAYS, BANNS, AND EXCOMMUNICATIONS

No mention of these is made, another indication of the Puritan character of this revision.

OFFERTORY SENTENCES

Tobit iv, 8 and 9 are retained by Wesley.

PRAYER FOR THE WHOLE STATE OF CHRIST'S CHURCH

The word 'oblations' is retained.

THE THREE EXHORTATIONS

These are removed. Wesley seeks to shorten this service, and the exhortations served no useful purpose. Early Methodists were so rigorously disciplined in their Societies, that there was little danger of unrepentant sinners receiving.

GENERAL CONFESSION

The words, 'the burden of them is intolerable' are deleted.

ABSOLUTION

The name 'Absolution' is omitted. It is changed into a prayer, 'O Almighty God . . . Have mercy upon us . . .', etc.

PROPER PREFACE

The proper preface for Christmas Day omits, 'the substance of the Virgin Mary his mother'.

PRAYER OF CONSECRATION

The manual acts are included. It was not until 1864 that Methodist opinion removed them from this service. But some Methodist ministers have always retained them.

Wesley deletes from the rubric the words, 'all meekly kneeling'. The Rev. Frederick Hunter recalls that Wesley did not require Dissenters to kneel at the Tabernacle, Norwich, in 1759. He preferred the practice, but would not enforce it (*Journal*, IV, p. 302). The Presbyterians in 1661 had objected to kneeling, because it 'would oblige them to reject all such from the Communion as would not receive it kneeling' (Calamy).

Editions of this service vary. In some, Ante-Communion vanishes completely, or alternates with Morning Prayer. It is interesting to note that Dr. Rattenbury states that the placing of the Prayer of Oblation before Communion, in the manner of the Deposited Book, would be unacceptable to Methodists, as suggesting the idea of sacrifice.

Wesley's office permits the Elder to pray extempore before the blessing. Extemporary prayer was a Methodist innovation, though the Presbyterian divines in 1661 had sought some latitude for free prayer in church services. It will be observed that the rubric forbidding a celebration save in the presence of three communicants is abandoned. No Methodist minister would think of celebrating Communion by himself!

PUBLIC BAPTISM OF INFANTS

This office is called, 'The Ministration of Baptism of Infants'. It eliminates sponsors. At the Savoy Conference the Presbyterians had declared that, in their opinion, the parents were the fittest both to dedicate the child unto God, and to covenant for it.

The declaration, 'It is certain by God's Word, that children which are baptized, dying before they commit actual sin, are undoubtedly saved', is not included. It had given great offence to the Presbyterians at the Savoy. They had maintained that there was no certainty by God's Word, at the most only a probable deduction from it. Baxter himself was of the opinion 'that of the forty sinful terms for a communion with the Church party, if thirty-nine were taken away, and only that rubric, concerning the salvation of infants dying shortly after their baptism, were continued, yet they could not conform'.

The Exhortation is retained intact, including the words 'born anew of water'. But the words in the first prayer, 'didst sanctify water to the mystical washing away of sin', are changed to 'didst sanctify water for this holy sacrament'. The Presbyterians had objected to the notion of the sanctification of Jordan, or any other waters, to a sacramental use by Christ's baptism. The second prayer, 'Almighty and Immortal God', which contains the sentence 'may receive remission of his sins by spiritual regeneration', is omitted.

The Exhortation on the Gospel and the Thanksgiving Prayer are omitted, probably for brevity. The Address to the Sponsors and the vicarious stipulations are removed. On this question the Presbyterians at the Savoy had spoken forcibly. 'We know not by what right the sureties do promise and answer in the name of the infant.'

The prayer, 'Almighty, everliving God' is included, but omits the sanctification of the water. Mr. Wesley allows sprinkling as well as immersion and affusion. Thus, '. . . he shall dip it in the water, or pour water upon it, or sprinkle it therewith'. This may be the first reference in any baptismal rite to the use of sprinkling as a valid mode of Baptism. Dr. Darwell Stone observes in his *Holy Baptism* (p. 135) that 'while, failing immersion, it is greatly to be desired that the water be poured and not sprinkled, all Western theologians agree that if water is made to flow upon the head of the baptised person the baptism is valid'.

The sign of the cross, and the reception are removed. Objection to the signation was an old Puritan grievance. Its abolition was asked for at Hampton Court and at the Savoy. The Royal Commission of 1689 proposed to retain its usage as an 'ancient and laudable custom of the Church', though refuting the idea that 'using that sign is of any virtue or efficacy of itself'. The Commission was prepared to make provision for ministers with conscientious scruples.

The Exhortation to Thanksgiving does not include 'this child is regenerate'. The Thanksgiving Prayer is altered to, 'We yield thee hearty thanks, most merciful Father, that it hath pleased thee to receive this infant for thine own child by adoption, and to admit him into thy holy Church.' The Presbyterians in 1661 had maintained that 'we cannot in faith say that every child that is baptised is "regenerated by God's Holy Spirit".' A concluding extemporary prayer is allowed.

PRIVATE BAPTISM

This office is expunged, as would be expected in a Puritan revision.

BAPTISM TO SUCH AS ARE OF RIPER YEARS

No further change of importance. The Exhortation on the Gospel is removed for brevity. The candidates answer the interrogatories for themselves. The reception and signation are removed. Wesley omits the words, 'are regenerate' from the Exhortation to Thanksgiving Prayer, and 'now' from 'being now born again', in the Prayer.

CONFIRMATION

This order is not included, another indication of the Puritan tradition.

HOLY MATRIMONY

The use of the ring is expunged. This is a further instance of Wesley's Puritanism. It was restored in 1846. It was restored, and made optional, in the American Methodist Episcopal Church in 1864, and in the American Episcopal Church, South, in 1866. The use of one, or two, rings is permitted, not required, in the current discipline of the Methodist Church (U.S.A.). Wesley omits the words, 'with my body I thee worship'. He excludes all reference to the ring.

VISITATION OF THE SICK

This office is not included. The Presbyterians at the Savoy had objected to the Absolution. They desired it should be made 'declarative and conditional', such as, 'I pronounce thee absolved . . . if thou dost truly repent and believe.'

COMMUNION OF THE SICK

No change of importance. The rubrics are omitted, save for the rubric directing that the sick person should communicate last. This office last appears in the 1842 edition.

BURIAL OF THE DEAD

This service is much shortened, and the first rubric omitted. Methodist clergy exclude none from Christian burial. The commendation and the preceding rubric are removed, another instance of Puritan influence. At the Savoy the Presbyterians had objected to the clause, 'to take unto Himself', on the ground that it 'cannot in truth be said of persons living and dying in open and notorious sin'. The prayer, 'Almighty God', is deleted. From the collect are excluded the words, 'as our hope is this our brother doth'. This change is in the Puritan tradition.

CHURCHING OF WOMEN

This office is not included, another instance of Wesley's Puritanism.

A COMMINATION

This office is not included.

THE PSALMS

Many psalms are removed, and others abridged, 'as being highly improper for the mouths of a Christian Congregation'. Dr. Rattenbury in his book deplores the fact that the use of psalms and canticles in Methodism is disappearing.

FORMS OF PRAYER TO BE USED AT SEA; GUNPOWDER TREASON; KING CHARLES THE MARTYR; THE RESTORATION

These offices are not included.

49

THE ORDAINING OF DEACONS

In this service, which closely follows the Prayer Book, the Superintendent lays hands on the ordinand, and gives him the Bible. He says, 'Take thou authority to read the Holy Scriptures, in the Church of God, and to preach the same.'

THE ORDAINING OF ELDERS

This service closely follows the Prayer Book. The Superintendent and Elders present lay on hands. The Superintendent says: 'Receive the Holy Ghost for the Office and Work of an Elder in the Church of God, now committed unto thee by the imposition of our hands. And be thou a faithful Dispenser of the Word of God, and of his holy Sacraments; in the Name . . . etc.' No commission is given to give absolution. The Superintendent delivers the Bible, with the words, 'Take thou authority to preach the Word of God, and to administer the holy Sacraments in the Congregation.'

THE ORDINATION OF SUPERINTENDENTS

This service closely follows the Prayer Book. The Superintendent and Elders lay on hands. The Superintendent says: 'Receive the Holy Ghost for the office and work of a Superintendent in the Church of God, now committed unto thee by the imposition of our hands; in the name of the Father, and of the Son, and of the Holy Ghost. Amen. And remember that thou stir up the grace of God which is given thee by this imposition of our hands; for God hath not given us the spirit of fear, but of power, and love, and soberness.' The Superintendent delivers the Bible with the customary words. The reader will appreciate that, although the word 'bishop' does not appear in this ordinal, this service was the means whereby American Methodism was committed to an episcopal form of Church government. But Methodist bishops belong to the same order as presbyters. In his famous letter to Asbury (20th September 1788), Wesley exclaimed: 'Men may call me a knave, a fool, a rascal, a scoundrel, and I am content; but they shall

never by my consent call me a bishop.' Wesley omits from the
presentation of the bishop-elect the qualification 'well-learned'.
Not academic but spiritual ability is the sole desideratum.
American bishops wear no special episcopal habit. Nor do
their clergy wear cassocks and surplices. But in England the
Geneva gown, with or without cassock, is very common.

It is to be noted that the Methodist clergy testify to their
acceptance of the Holy Scriptures, and to the doctrine of 'the
first four volumes of Mr. Wesley's sermons and his notes on the
New Testament'.

THE TWENTY-FIVE ARTICLES

Wesley reduces the number of the Thirty-Nine Articles to
Twenty-Five by omissions and abbreviations. His purpose was
to eliminate Calvinism. Methodism has been described as,
'Arminianism set on fire'. The following Articles are expunged:
Nos. VIII (the Three Creeds); XIII (Works before Justifica-
tion); XV (Christ alone without sin); XVII (Predestination
and Election); XVIII (Salvation only by the name of Christ);
XX; XXI (Authority of the Church and General Councils);
XXIII (The Ministry); XXVI (Unworthy ministers and the
Sacrament); XXIX (Of the Wicked); XXXIII (Excom-
munications); XXXV (Homilies); XXXVI (Consecrations
and Ordinations); The title of XVI is changed from 'Sin after
Baptism', to 'Sin after Justification'. Article XXVII (of
Baptism) is retained but shortened, reference to impartation of
grace being omitted. The word 'ministers' is substituted for
Bishops, priests and deacons in XXXII. The title of Article
XXXIV is changed from 'Traditions of the Church', to 'Rites
and Ceremonies of Churches'. Article IX (Original Sin) is cut
down, for Wesley held that his doctrine of sanctification was
in conflict with 'this infection of nature doth remain'. It is to be
noted that Wesley omits Article III, 'Of the going down of
Christ into Hell'. The clause, 'He descended into hell', was
omitted by most Semi-Arian revisers of the Prayer Book in the
eighteenth century as unscriptural. No mention is made of the
Apocrypha in Article VI. This provides another link with
Puritanism. Article XXXVII (Civil Magistrates) is curtailed
to set aside the principle of State-establishment.

The late Dr. Duncan Coomer was wont to remark on Wesley's 'curious predilection for abridgements'. Not only did he abridge the Prayer Book but the Shorter Catechism and the *Pilgrim's Progress*! But Wesley's 'Abridgement' of the Prayer Book was something more than a simplification. It was a revision, and a Puritan revision. That this is so the above analysis has sought to demonstrate. Wesley's High Church upbringing may have obscured his Puritan ancestry. But it would be unwise to forget that his mother's father, Dr. Annesley, was one of the 'ejected clergy' of 1662. It is significant that in a letter to his friend the Rev. Samuel Walker of Truro, written on the 20th November 1755, Wesley should have commented on the criticisms of the Prayer Book made by the Puritans in 1662. 'I myself so far allow the force of several of those objections, that I should not dare to declare my Assent and Consent to that Book in the Terms prescribed. Indeed they are so strong, that I think they cannot safely be used, with regard to any Book but ye Bible.' In an article in the *Proceedings of the Wesley Historical Society* (June, 1942) the Rev. Frederick Hunter maintains that Wesley's revision was inspired by the proposals of the Presbyterians at the Savoy Conference. It is Mr. Hunter's contention that Wesley was led to make a revision of this kind by reading Calamy's *Abridgement of Mr. Baxter's History of His Life and Times*. Wesley read this book in April, 1754 (*Journal* IV, p. 93). It is certain it made a deep impression upon his mind. This was his comment. 'In spite of all the prejudices of education, I could not but see that the poor Nonconformists had been used without either justice or mercy; and that many of the Protestant Bishops of King Charles had neither more religion, nor humanity, than the Popish Bishops of Queen Mary.' In his letter to Samuel Walker (*Letters* III, p. 152), Wesley very particularly summarised Chapter 10 of Calamy. Mr. Hunter believes that Wesley formulated his revision of the Prayer Book with Calamy's book before him, and concludes: 'His revisions were dictated by love of that "Baxterian" Church of England, which would have comprehended at least his Presbyterian and perhaps also his Congregational ancestors.' It may not be possible to assess to a precise degree this undoubted Puritan influence. Certainly, Wesley revised the Prayer Book not by additions, but by omissions. But he was no revolutionary. He preserved as much as he could. Referring to his 'Abridgement' in a letter from Dublin of the 20th June 1789, he wrote: 'I took particular care throughout to alter nothing for altering's sake. In religion I am for as few innovations as possible. I love the old wine best.'

It has been observed that the first edition of Wesley's 'Abridgement' was published in 1784 for the new United States. It was entitled: *The Sunday Service of the Methodists in North America with other Occasional Services*, and was printed in London. Until recently, the only known copy of the edition was to be found in the library of Drew University, New Jersey, U.S.A. At the present time twenty-three copies are extant, all in the United States or Canada. The fourth and last edition of this 'Abridgement' to be published for the United States in London appeared in 1790. As originally prepared by Wesley this book contained twenty-four of the thirty-nine Articles of the Church of England. But the Christmas Conference held at Baltimore in 1784 added a further article in respect to the civil rulers of America, and the second edition of the prayer book, *The Sunday Service of the Methodists in the United States of America, with Other Occasional Services*, published in 1786, had twenty-five articles. The *Sunday Service for the Methodists in North America*, survived only to 1792. As the Methodist Bishop Cooke was to write in his *History of the Ritual*: 'It was not the genius of Methodism to be confined to forms.' But although the Sunday liturgical service disappeared from American Methodism, Holy Communion and the 'occasional services' as prepared by Wesley were retained, with modifications, in both the Methodist Episcopal Church, and the Methodist Episcopal Church, South. Thus the Prayer Book is still most influential in American Methodism.

The American revision omits the Royal Prayers but these are included in *The Sunday Service of the Methodists in His Majesty's Dominions*, issued in 1786. Already was Methodism established in Newfoundland, Nova Scotia, and Antigua.

It was in 1786 that the first edition of Wesley's 'Abridgement' was published for this country. It was called, *The Sunday Service of the Methodists; with other Occasional Services*. Even this edition gives rise to problems. It is true that such names as 'U.S.A.' or 'H.M. Dominions' are dropped from the title page. But

Mr. Wesley F. Swift was not persuaded that the edition was intended primarily for England. At this time no Methodist service was permitted in church hours, and Methodists were expected to attend Parish Church services. Moreover, during Wesley's lifetime, Holy Communion was administered in a very small number of chapels, and by ordained clergymen only. The fact remains, it was under this name that the liturgy continued to be reissued during the greater part of the nineteenth century. Editions were published in 1788, 1792, 1812, 1816, 1817, 1819, 1825, 1826, 1834, 1837, 1838, 1841, 1842, 1846, 1849, 1852, 1857, 1859, 1860, 1861, 1863, 1873, 1876, 1878, and seven undated editions between 1846 and 1910. Thus over thirty editions were published for use in Great Britain until its final appearance in 1910. Furthermore, between 1839 and 1881 there appeared at least fifteen editions of a shorter 'Book of Offices' under the title, *Order of Administration of the Sacraments and Other Services, for the use of the People called Methodists*, making a total of at least forty-five editions.

It will be observed that the title of Wesley's 'Abridgement' is *The Sunday Service*. This was a departure from the Anglican conception of Morning and Evening Prayer as daily services. Although Wesley directed that his travelling preachers should read the Litany on Wednesdays and Fridays, he expected them to pray extempore on all other days. For Wesley was indebted not only to Anglicanism but to the primitive Christian Church, and the Moravian Societies. As long as he lived, the Prayer Book retained a sure place in Methodist worship. But even he considered it defective. In a letter to Samuel Walker of the 20th November 1755, he confessed: 'Neither dare I confine myself wholly to Forms of Prayer, not even in the Church. I use indeed all ye Forms; but I frequently add extemporary Prayer, either before or after Sermon.' Wesley's devotion to the Prayer Book was not shared by very many Methodists, even in his lifetime. The majority of his converts were recruited from outside the churches. They loved their Founder more than his prayer book and were not unwilling to let it go. When the Plan of Pacification was formulated in 1795 a clause was included which, in effect, left the use of the liturgy optional. 'Wherever Divine Service is performed in England, on the Lord's Day in Church-hours, the officiating Preacher shall read either the Service of the Established Church, our venerable father's Abridgement, or at least, the Lessons appointed by the Calendar.'

The Prayer Book or Wesley's 'Abridgement' was adopted by London and some of the larger towns. But in general the societies in rural areas dispensed with a liturgy. In some industrial towns the circuit itself was divided. In Halifax the urban chapels favoured the 'Abridgement', and the country chapels non-liturgical services. During the nineteenth century the use of the liturgy declined, though as late as 1874 prayer book worship was observed in most of the London churches. The building of neo-Gothic chapels brought a spasmodic revival. It is interesting to note that at the handsome Trinity Methodist Church, Southport, so much admired by Ruskin, liturgical worship continues. In present-day Methodism less than forty churches use the liturgy regularly, and almost half of these are in London. One curious fact deserves notice. At all times Methodists have preferred the original Prayer Book to the 'Abridgement'. In modern Methodism more than half the liturgical churches use the Church of England edition.

But Wesley's 'Abridgement' is not a pious relic. It has achieved a resounding success on the mission field, and is most popular with native congregations. This fact explains the astonishing number of editions. Missionaries found the 'Abridgement' most convenient when educating their converts to accept an ordered form of worship. In this way many native congregations developed a preference for liturgical worship.

It is evident that a Sunday liturgy has never moved the soul of British Methodism. But there is something touching in the continued use of a prayer book at Wesley's Chapel, London, and at the annual Conference Service. It is a tribute to the beloved father-in-God who loved the liturgy all his days, and a deeper tribute of devotion to the Church of England as the 'Mother Church of Methodism'.

The influence of the Prayer Book in Great Britain and America was to survive in the Holy Communion and occasional services. Revisions of these services show a sturdy independency of thought. Never have Methodists given to their founder a blind devotion. Dr. Church has pointed to the formative influence of the early Methodist people. And Wesley himself, the noblest of the Benevolent Despots of the eighteenth century, was always sensitive to the public opinion of his societies.

The early Methodists were trained to regard Holy Communion as the central act of worship. Methodist celebrations were permitted under the Plan of Pacification, and gradually became customary. The Rev. Wesley F. Swift, in a highly informative article in the *Proceedings of the Wesley Historical Society*, for June 1949, comments on the many attempts to tamper with the 'Abridgement' prior to 1882. 'The "manual acts" in the Communion Office', he says, 'appear and disappear in successive editions after the manner of the famous Cheshire Cat and for no obvious reason.' In America, the manual acts do not appear in the first edition of 1784, which has provided a problem for American scholars. But they are included in the 1792 and succeeding Disciplines. They were discarded by the Methodist Episcopal Church, South, in 1854, but were retained by the Methodist Episcopal Church. In 1939, when the Methodist Episcopal Church, the Methodist Episcopal Church, South, and the Methodist Protestant Church united to form the Methodist Church, they were made optional. They were relinquished by British Methodism in 1864. There is no doubt, however, that Wesley intended the manual acts to be used. They are included in the 1786 edition of *The Sunday Service of the Methodists* in John Rylands Library. It is incredible that Wesley, always something of the High Churchman, should have made an omission so momentous without supplying some justification.

The truth would seem to be that the Methodist conscience was not satisfied. Hence the repeated efforts to drop the manual acts in both England and America. The learned Dr. Summers of the American Episcopal Church, South, gave the explanation. 'As the handling of the bread and wine required by the old rubrics while reciting this prayer is considered by some a mimicry of our Saviour's sacrifice—the offering of him as an unbloody sacrifice upon the altar—our Church expunged the rubrics requiring it.'

It was in 1840 that the Conference at Newcastle-upon-Tyne insisted that baptism should be administered in liturgical form. But the Methodist mind was much exercised about this office.

For as Dr. Church has written: 'It is probably true to say that John Wesley was more vague in his teaching on Baptism, especially infant baptism, than on any other subject.' High Churchman and Evangelical were at variance here in the man. As a sacramentalist he stressed the efficacy of this sacrament. His *Treatise on Baptism*, published in 1756, echoed the words of his father's 'Pious Communicant Rightly Prepar'd'. But the Evangelical in Wesley cried in his sermon on the 'Marks of the New Birth', 'Say not in your heart, I was once baptized, therefore I am now a child of God. Alas, that consequence will by no means hold. How many are the baptized gluttons and drunkards, the baptized liars and common swearers, the baptized railers and evil speakers, the baptized whoremongers, thieves, extortioners? What think you? Are these now the children of God? Verily I say unto you, whosoever you are, unto whom any of the preceding characters belong, "Ye are of your father the devil, and the works of your father ye do".' English and American Methodists found this attitude confusing. It was an American Methodist who said that the baptismal office 'squints at baptismal regeneration'. In England the Oxford Movement made Methodists aware that it was the Prayer Book that was 'the seed-plot of all the Romanising errors which now distract and menace the Church of England' (*The Methodist Recorder*, 1874, p. 490.). There were loud cries against 'born anew of water', and the 'mystical washing away of sin'. A long controversy was ended only by the publication in 1882 of a new revision by authority of the Conference.

Decisions of importance were made by the Wesleyan Methodists in the nineteenth century. By 1848 the Ordinal had become the 'Form of Ordaining Candidates for the Ministry in the Wesleyan Methodist Connexion', a revision based largely on Wesley's 'Form and Manner of Ordaining of Elders'. In 1864 it was agreed that the Burial of the Dead should be conducted according to liturgical forms. But the most momentous decision was the publication, by authority of the Conference, of *The Book of Public Prayers and Services for the use of the People called Methodists*, in 1882. The new book was hailed with enthusiasm. Mr. Wesley F. Swift, who examined the lengthy Conference debates of that time, says that few speakers had a good word for Wesley's 'Abridgement'. With the publication of the new liturgy a long controversy, mainly focused on the Baptismal office, was brought to a close.

The Book of Public Prayers and Services includes an order for Morning Prayer that is but a slight revision of the Anglican Prayer Book. The names 'Epiphany', 'Septuagesima', and 'Lent', are reinserted. The Psalter is taken from the Bible, and not from the Prayer Book. The Communion office is a somewhat closer approximation to the Prayer Book than is Wesley's 'Abridgement'. Thus the Nicene Creed is restored, though the offertory sentences from Tobit are expunged. An abbreviated third exhortation is included. The manual acts are not preserved. The Ministration of Baptism to Infants departs considerably from the Prayer Book. The words, 'mystical washing away of sin', do not occur. The signation is not included. The ring is retained in the Marriage Service. The Burial Service includes the commendation in the form, 'Forasmuch as it hath pleased Almighty God to call hence the soul of our dear brother here departed, we therefore commit his body to the ground; earth to earth, ashes to ashes, dust to dust; in sure and certain hope that the dead in Christ shall rise to everlasting life . . . etc.' The words 'as our hope is this our brother doth', are dropped from the collect, 'O merciful God'. The Form of Ordaining Candidates for the Ministry is based on Wesley's form for ordaining elders. No distinction is made between deacon, presbyter, and superintendent as in Wesley's 'Abridgement'. Candidates testify to their acceptance of the system of doctrine contained in the first four volumes of Mr. Wesley's sermons, and his notes on the New Testament. Hands are laid on with the words, 'Mayest thou receive the Holy Ghost', etc. This liturgy includes forms for the 'Setting Apart of Deaconesses', for 'Covenanting with God', and for the 'Public Recognition of New Members'.

The expansion of Methodism in the nineteenth century was but little impeded by the serious domestic disputes that led to separations from the parent body. For at no time was there controversy on vital theological issues. Some of the laity claimed a greater share in the government of the Church, and these champions of democracy did not hesitate to defy the Wesleyan 'priestocracy'. Among the seceders were the Primitive Methodists (1808); the Bible Christians (1815); and the United

Methodist Free Church (1857). But these melancholy divisions proved a passing phase. In 1907 the Methodist New Connexion (1797) united with the Bible Christians and the United Methodist Free Church to form the United Methodist Church. Methodist reunion was completed in 1932 when Wesleyan Methodists, Primitive Methodists, and United Methodists joined together in the one Methodist Church.

It was not until 1860 that the Primitive Methodists, always more emotional than the Wesleyan Methodists, issued 'Forms for the Administration of Baptism; the Solemnization of Matrimony; Maternal thanksgiving after child-birth; Administration of the Lord's Supper; Renewing our Covenant with God; and for the Burial of the dead.' This book is in the British Museum. The services are very 'Nonconformist' in character, though indebted in some degree to the Prayer Book. Thus a prayer in the Baptismal Service contains reference to Noah, the Red Sea, and the baptism of Christ in Jordan. Reception of the Bread and Wine at the Lord's Supper is permitted, 'at the communion rails, or in the pews, sitting or kneeling, as may be most convenient or agreeable to the respective societies'. Sometime after 1890 the Primitive Methodists issued an 'Order of Administration of Baptism and Other Services'. The services for the Baptism of Infants and for Such as are of Riper Years are not unlike those contained in *The Book of Public Prayers and Services*, save that the word 'sacrament' is replaced by 'ordinance'. The sign of the cross is not made. The Marriage Service is not dissimilar to the one in *The Book of Public Prayers and Services*. The ring is given. The liturgy contains a prayer for Maternal Thanksgiving after child-birth. It is intended to be used before the concluding prayer at Sunday worship. The Burial Service is not unlike the service in *The Book of Public Prayers and Services*. The order for the Lord's Supper begins with a hymn and a prayer for the Church, followed by Scripture passages and exhortation (an abridged variation of the third exhortation in the Prayer Book, but with the words 'holy mysteries' changed to 'ordinance'). The general confession from the Prayer Book follows, being succeeded by the comfortable words through the omission of the Absolution. There follows an abridgement of the Anglican prayer of consecration, from which are expunged the words of institution and the manual acts. The office concludes with the words of delivery, a hymn, the prayer of oblation from the Prayer Book and the blessing. The liturgy includes a Covenant Service.

It would seem that the United Methodists published two books of occasional services. The second was entitled, *Book of Services for the use of the United Methodist Free Churches*. It would appear from the preface that this later book was a revision of the former but with a shorter Covenant Service, some longer occasional services, and an additional service for the recognition of new members. The United Methodist liturgy owes little to the Prayer Book. It is an attempt to give to ministers, used to free services, printed services of a rather more formal nature. Thus the address in the Lord's Supper may well be an original composition. It is noteworthy that the orders for the Baptism of Children and Adults refer to Baptism as an 'ordinance'. The sign of the cross is not used. In Adult Baptism the person to be baptized expresses belief in the Apostles' Creed and personal acceptance of Christ as Saviour. The order of the Lord's Supper begins with a hymn and a prayer followed by the Lord's Prayer. There follow portions of Scripture relating to the Last Supper, an address, a hymn, words of delivery, silent prayer, the offertory, a hymn and a concluding prayer. The Marriage Service includes the ring. The Burial Service closely resembles the office in *The Book of Public Prayers and Services*. The Ordination Service bears no resemblance to the Prayer Book. There is no laying on of hands. The concluding rubric states that 'the Reception of the candidates should be moved and seconded, and the representatives present asked to express their concurrence'.

The Bible Christian Church was a small offshoot of Methodism chiefly confined to the West of England. In the preface to the new edition of the *Book of Services for the Use of the Bible Christian Church* (1903) acknowledgements are made to the *Book of Services* of the United Methodist Free Churches, also to Dr. Condor's Marriage Service. The services in this liturgy are simple and short. In the Baptism services the sign of the cross is not used. A rubric at the beginning of the form for the Lord's Supper declares that 'whenever it can possibly be arranged, the Sacrament of the Lord's Supper shall be celebrated on the first Sunday in every month'. The Bible Christians

boldly use the word 'sacrament'. The office begins with Scripture passages, and hymn. Communicants are directed to kneel.
A prayer follows, together with St. Paul's account of the Last
Supper. An address is succeeded by the brief exhortation to
confession of sins from the Prayer Book. The words of delivery
are followed by prayer and blessing. The ring is used in the
Marriage Service. The commendation in the Burial Service
preserves the words of the Prayer Book, 'to take unto Himself
the soul of our dear brother here departed'. The liturgy contains a service for the Recognition of New Members, a Covenant
Service, incorporating the general confession from Anglican
Morning Prayer, and a Service for the Public Reception of
Ministers into full Connexion. Ministerial recognition is en-
dorsed by a show of hands of the congregation.

A *Book of Services for the Use of the United Methodist Church* was
published in 1913, by direction of the Conference. It is an able
production, with excellent prayers. This book is not in the
Prayer Book tradition. The sign of the cross is absent from
Baptism, but the ring is used in the Marriage Service. The
Communion office begins with Scripture sentences, hymns, and
Lord's Prayer. A prayer of thanksgiving follows, with a reading
from a Gospel or Epistle, and hymn and offertory. The words
of institution follow without the manual acts. After the words
of delivery there is a prayer, parting hymn, and blessing. Other
services contained in this liturgy are for the Recognition of
New Members, a Covenant Service, an order for the Recognition of Local Preachers, and an order for the Public Ordination
of Ministers received into full Connexion. In this service the
President reminds the ordinands that they are not priests, but
Methodist preachers, and that their office 'is the noblest of
callings'. The ordinand, after briefly relating his conversion, is
given the Bible, and the Veni, Creator is sung. There is no
laying on of hands. There is also an order for the Public Ordination of Non-Ministerial Foreign Missionaries. The commendation in the Burial Service is altered to 'call hence the soul of our
dear brother here departed'. The words 'as our hope is this our
brother doth', are retained in the collect, 'O merciful God!'

In 1930 the Wesleyan Methodist Conference appointed a
committee of ministers and laymen 'to consider the best
methods of giving to corporate prayer its due place in the life

of the Church'. The report of this committee, which was presented to the first united conference of the Methodist Church, stated that there were signs among the Methodist people that the guidance of the Holy Spirit pointed towards the wisdom of blending extemporary with directed and responsive prayer. It was as a consequence of this report that *Divine Worship* was published in 1935. This liturgy consists of ten orders of worship, and special orders for Christmas Day, Good Friday, Easter Morning and Whit Sunday. It includes a responsive service for children, and responsive acts of worship illustrating such themes as the life of the Church, the social life of the community, and the Christian life. The litanies of Dr. John Hunter are employed here to good purpose. *Divine Worship* is of interest because the editors have seen fit to introduce to Methodism a type of service that is finding considerable favour among Congregationalists. These services are not rigidly constructed. They make provision for extemporary and silent prayer, and allow a congregation a large measure of vocal participation in worship, by means of litanies and responsive acts. As the Introduction to *Divine Worship* observes, 'the value of responsive worship is finding increasing recognition amongst the Free Churches. The present book is only one of a succession of manuals of public worship which have been published in recent years'. It remains to be seen whether Methodists will take kindly to this innovation. It would not appear that *Divine Worship* is widely used. Prayers in this book are taken from the Prayer Book, *A Book of Congregational Worship*, the *Directory of Public Worship*, the *New Church Liturgy*, the *Free Church Book of Common Prayer*, and the prayers of Martineau. *Divine Worship* maintains an historic link with Wesley by the inclusion of a slight adaptation of Anglican Morning Prayer. Variations of this service are provided, based on the Deposited Book. The liturgy for Trinity Methodist Church, Southport, makes similar changes.

The Book of Offices being the Orders of Service authorised for use in the Methodist Church was issued in 1936. No attempt is made to disparage free prayer, always 'one of the glories of Methodism'. An express place for extemporary prayer is provided in many of the services. The office for Morning Prayer is a much closer approximation to the Prayer Book than is Wesley's 'Abridgement', though the prayer used by Wesley in place of the Absolution is retained, and the Prayer Book Absolution is amended as follows, 'Almighty God . . . hath given commandment to his Ministers to declare unto all men, being penitent, the remission of their sins through faith in our Lord Jesus Christ.' The Benedicite is not included, but the title is restored to 'A Prayer of St. Chrysostom'. A note to the Apostles' Creed explains hell as hades or the world of spirits, very much in the manner of Semi-Arian revisions. The Collects, Epistles, and Gospels faithfully follow the Prayer Book, save that all Saints' Days are omitted, together with the Circumcision of Christ, Ash Wednesday, Maundy Thursday, the Conversion of Saint Paul, the Purification of Saint Mary, and the Annunciation of the Virgin Mary. It is noteworthy that the order of the Lord's Supper is also entitled in this book, 'The Holy Communion'. This service follows the Prayer Book very closely. Nevertheless the celebrant is given full liberty to use hymns and extemporary prayer. The offertory sentences from the Apocrypha, retained by Wesley, are not used. But Wesley's prayer to displace the Absolution is preserved, along with his proper preface for Christmas Day. The manual acts are not included. The Nicene Creed, omitted by Wesley, is included, and the words 'holy Sacrament' are employed. This office incorporates some of the features of the Deposited Book. Thus our Lord's Summary of the Law is permitted as an alternative to the Ten Commandments; the proper preface for All Saints' Day is included, but no collect, and the words 'New Covenant' replace 'New Testament' in the prayer of consecration. *The Book of Offices* contains an alternative Communion order. This is a simpler service designed after Methodist Union for those Methodist churches which had been used to simple celebrations. Services of Infant and Adult Baptism are included. Unlike the Methodist Episcopal Church and the Methodist Episcopal Church, South, the English Methodist Church has not reintroduced sponsors. Nor has the signation been restored. An order of Thanksgiving of Mothers on the occasion of the birth of a child is included, together with an order for the Public Reception of New Members. A note in this liturgy recalls 25th December 1747, when John Wesley urged his Methodists to renew their covenant with God. The Covenant service includes acts of

Adoration, Thanksgiving and Confession, in the form of responses by minister and people. The Ordination of Candidates
for the Ministry is based on the orders of ordination and consecration in the Prayer Book. Candidates are ordained by the
laying on of hands by the President and other ministers, with
the words, 'Mayest thou receive the Holy Spirit for the office
and work of a Christian Minister and Pastor, now committed
unto thee by the imposition of our hands. And be thou a
faithful Dispenser of the Word of God, and of His holy Sacraments, in the name of the Father . . .' etc. There are also
services for the Ordination of Deaconesses, the Recognition of
Local Preachers, and the Dedication of Sunday School Teachers.
The Marriage Service contains the words, 'With this Ring, a
token and pledge of the Vow and Covenant now made betwixt
me and thee, I thee wed, in the Name of the Father . . .' etc.
The commendation in the Burial Service includes the words,
'to take unto Himself the soul of our dear brother here departed'. But the words, 'as our hope is this our brother doth', are
not restored to the collect.

The Confirmation office, restored by the Methodist Episcopal Church, in 1864, and by the Methodist Episcopal Church,
South, in 1870, has not been reintroduced to British Methodism.

It would appear from this survey that the liturgical tradition
in Methodism remains of considerable importance. This is the
more surprising as so few chapels retain liturgical Sunday
worship. Not only Wesleyan Methodists but Primitive Methodists, United Methodists, and Bible Christians have discovered
a need for liturgical use in occasional services. But it is to
Wesleyan Methodism that liturgical worship has made the
surest appeal. This is explained by an Anglican parentage.
Wesleyan Methodism cherishes a Church of England ancestry.
The origin of the other Methodist bodies is very different. Thus
the early Primitive Methodists were led by two local preachers,
Hugh Bourne and William Clowes, who had come under the
influence of an American Methodist, Laurence Dow. The
Methodist Conference was hostile to their camp-meetings, as an
unseemly American innovation. Hence the formation of the
Primitive Methodist Connexion. The Bible Christians owe their
beginnings to a Cornish local preacher, William O'Bryan. He
was severely disciplined in Cornwall for irregular evangelism.

The liturgical tradition in Methodism is of something more than academic interest. It is a long tradition. It has excited the interest and stirred the emotions of Methodists from Wesley's day to our own. It may be true to say that the Methodist mind is increasingly sacramental. The Anglican tradition survives.

CHAPTER IV

THE COUNTESS OF HUNTINGDON'S CONNEXION

IT was in satiric vein that Horace Walpole dubbed Selina, Countess of Huntingdon, 'Queen of the Methodists'. But a kinder and shrewder estimate was that of Cardinal Newman. He said of her: 'She devoted herself, her name, her means, her time, her thoughts to the cause of Christ. She acted as one ought to act who considered this life a pilgrimage, not a home.' Possibly the memory of Selina has suffered because she was so very much the *grande dame*. In her own day her evangelical enthusiasm shocked Society. The Duchess of Buckingham was much provoked. It was monstrous to tell a lady of rank her heart was as sinful as a common wretch's. On the other hand, the more democratic instincts of our day are repelled by an autocratic handling of church affairs. But the authority of the Countess in her Connexion was little different from that of Wesley in his.

It was with some asperity that John Wesley referred to the followers of the Countess as 'the genteel Methodists'. But in an age when a Primate could entertain Society with balls at his palace, there was need of a mission to the upper classes. As George III said to one of his bishops: 'I wish there was a Lady Huntingdon in every diocese in the Kingdom.'

The Countess made the family seat Donington Park, Leicestershire, a centre of the Evangelical revival. Great cynics like Chesterfield and Bolingbroke attended her prayer meetings, and were moved by the dramatic passion of Whitefield's preaching. This great evangelist was one of her ladyship's chaplains. In her endeavour to infuse new life into the Church of England this 'noble and elect lady' offered generous hospitality to the clergy. She sold her jewels to build a chapel at Brighton. She travelled extensively for the gospel. She suffered abuse in the streets. Hooligans broke the windows of her Ashby home. Although George Whitefield is regarded as the apostle of Calvinistic Methodism, it was the Countess who organised a denomination.

Whitefield was a Calvinist. Hence his breach with Wesley on this issue in 1740. Two years later the friends were reconciled, and their personal devotion never wavered. Unfortunately the controversy came to a head again at the Methodist Conference of 1770. Lady Huntingdon championed the high Calvinists, insisting that no other views should be tolerated at her college at Trevecca. Fletcher of Madely thereupon withdrew.

John Wesley and Lady Huntington were at heart loyal Anglicans. But they were forced into Dissent to save their work. Lady Huntingdon exercised to the full her privilege as a peeress to appoint chaplains. But when she acquired Spa Fields Chapel the Incumbent of Clerkenwell successfully defended his authority in the parish. The existence of an important congregation was at stake. In 1781 the Countess with great reluctance seceded from the Church of England, and the minister of Spa Fields safeguarded his position by taking the oath of allegiance as a dissenting minister under the Toleration Act. Several of the clergy associated with the Countess now ceased to preach in her chapels. Two years later the secession was completed when six young men from Trevecca were set apart for the ministry at Spa Fields 'by the laying on of the hands of the Presbytery'.

It was the hope of Lady Huntingdon that her ministers should occupy a helpful neutrality between the Establishment and Dissent. Her Connexion was to interpret the doctrinal Articles of the Church of England in their strict Calvinistic sense, and to preserve Prayer Book worship. 'We desire', said Dr. Haweis, 'to be one with the Church of England.' This was not to be. Sixty-seven chapels existed at the secession. But the Countess died before their future had been determined. Wesley left behind him 'a legal hundred'. Had Lady Huntingdon made similar provision the history of her Connexion might have been very different.

In 1823 an Annual Conference was established. The 1847 Conference affirmed a detached position as to Church Order. 'Upon the ground of sacred Scripture, and from the earlier ecclesiastical records, it contends that many of the apostolical Churches varied in their internal structure; that hence the different orders of Congregational, Presbyterian, and Episcopal Churches do advocate their origin; and it argues that none of these varieties should form a barrier to the intercommunion of Churches.' From 1863–8 the Connexion was associated with the Free Church of England. Today most of the thirty-eight remaining churches are allied with the Congregationalists.

The Connexion was the first Protestant communion to undertake a Mission in Sierra Leone, and this work still flourishes. Probably the best known heritage of the Connexion is Cheshunt College, Cambridge, the healthy off-spring of Trevecca. The college is undenominational, but is closely connected with Congregationalism.

The older Calvinism is little stressed today in Lady Huntingdon's Chapels. A hundred years ago the Principal of Cheshunt College remarked that the old bitterness of the Calvinist-Arminian controversy was a thing of the past. More recently Dr. Harrison has pointed to "the curious paradox that . . . in the truest devotion and purest worship the controversy was transcended. At the Tabernacle (of Whitefield) and at the Foundry (of Wesley) both congregations could sing both 'Rock of Ages' of the Calvinist Toplady and 'Jesu, lover of my soul' of the Arminian Charles Wesley."

It will be appreciated that Lady Huntingdon's Connexion played a worthy part in a great epoch of history. And many must have echoed the words of George III: 'When I am dying, I think I shall be happy to seize the skirt of Lady Huntingdon's mantle, to lift me up with her to Heaven.'

It was the intention of Lady Huntingdon that the liturgy of the Church of England should be read in her chapels, and this continued to be the practice during her lifetime. After her death most of the chapels abandoned the Prayer Book, for the ordinary free service of Nonconformity. The fact was that the chapels were left very much to their own devices. The only restriction never relaxed was the need of all ministers to assent to the Calvinism of the fifteen doctrinal Articles.

Only four chapels, at Basingstoke, Brighton, Tunbridge Wells, and Worcester, still use the liturgy. But in the British Museum is a copy of a book especially published for the Tunbridge Wells congregation by the Rev. James Mountain in 1897. It is called *The Free Church Prayer Book*. In the preface Mountain explains that it had been his custom to use the Prayer Book. But he had felt the need of abbreviating the liturgy, introducing free prayer, and expunging sacerdotalism. His *Free Church Prayer Book* is based on the suggested revision of 1689, and the revised prayer books of John Wesley and Charles Stirling.[1] Thus he follows the lead taken by Stirling's *Protestant Prayer Book* of introducing into the prayer for the sovereign, 'Strengthen her that she may vanquish and overcome all the enemies of her throne and of the Protestant religion.' He also directs that the minister at Communion should stand behind the table, and that the prayer of humble access should read: 'Grant us, therefore, gracious Lord, so to commemorate, in the eating of this Bread and drinking of this Cup, the death of Thy dear Son Jesus Christ, that we may feed on Him in our hearts by faith.'

As regards rites and ceremonies, altar lights and the crucifix are not permitted by the Connexion. At Basingstoke, Brighton and Worcester the custom still survives for the minister to wear a surplice and to change to a black gown for the sermon. The surplice is resumed for Communion. This practice is not unknown in the Church of England.

The four chapels do not use a special revision of the Prayer Book. They use the Prayer Book with verbal alterations. In general the changes are as follows: The word 'absolution' is dropped, or the wording of the Absolution changed to, 'and hath promised to his people, being penitent, etc.'. 'Bishops and Curates' are replaced by 'Clergy and Ministers' or 'all Ministers of the Gospel', in the prayer for the Clergy and People. 'Christian Church' is sometimes substituted for the 'Catholick Church' in the prayer for all Conditions of Men. The Litany and Catechism are not used. At Basingstoke the Holy Communion office begins with the Invitation and ends with the *Gloria in Excelsis*. The Prayer Book is not often used for Burials, Weddings, or Infant Baptism. It is felt that these services do not express Free Church teaching.

[1] See Author's *Prayer Book Revisions of the Victorian Evangelicals*, pp. 14–26.

CHAPTER V

THE FREE CHURCH OF ENGLAND
OTHERWISE CALLED THE
REFORMED EPISCOPAL CHURCH

No Victorian bishop was more vigilant than Dr. Phill-potts, the great 'Harry of Exeter'. His was a brilliant mind, a caustic wit, and an almost ruthless sincerity. Such a man was a dangerous adversary to meet in the House of Lords or in his diocese of Exeter, over which he presided with despotic sway. Fierce hostility to the Evangelicals brought him into conflict with the Rev. James Shore, M.A., minister of Bridgetown Chapel-of-Ease, Totnes. Summarily and without explanation, Dr. Phillpotts withdrew this curate's licence. The chapel, which had been built by the Duke of Somerset for the use of his tenants, was closed. A few months later, as a result of representations made to the duke, the chapel was reopened. But the bishop's consent was still withheld when James Shore, who had already devoted himself to his congregation for ten years, resumed his ministry on 14th April 1844. On this date the Free Church of England may be said to have begun.

Dr. Phillpotts was not the man to accept so flagrant a con-tempt of his authority. But the situation at Totnes was peculiar. Bridgetown Chapel had never been consecrated. It seems cer-tain that Shore no longer regarded himself as a clergyman of the Church of England, although he continued to use the Prayer Book. He considered his church to be a free Church of England, free from episcopal supervision and jurisdiction. In the same year two other churches at Exeter and at Ilfra-combe were established as Free Church of England congrega-tions.

It has been seen how the Evangelical movement of the eighteenth century brought into being the Countess of Hun-tingdon's Connexion. This group of churches continued to adhere to the doctrines of grace in the Thirty-Nine Articles, and to some Prayer Book worship. The Connexion stretched forth the hand of fellowship to the Free Church of England. It was dangerous help. Shore accepted invitations to preach in Connexion chapels. The terrible bishop saw his chance and took it.

In considering the pathetic case of James Shore, it must in fairness be said that not the dignity alone, but the High Church principles of the bishop were affronted. Shore was still in holy orders. Phillpotts saw in him a rebel cleric, contumaciously conducting Nonconformist services. In 1849 he instituted proceedings against Shore in the ecclesiastical courts. The verdict went against the defendant who was ordered to pay costs. But Shore was a poor man. He could not pay. The hand of the bishop now moved heavily against him. On descending from the pulpit of the Countess of Huntingdon's Chapel at Spa Fields, he was arrested. For three months the Rev. James Shore was a prisoner in Exeter gaol.

It is not to be supposed that Shore's many sympathisers altogether appreciated the principles at issue. But their sense of fair play was offended by this uneven contest. Shore himself wrote to Thomas Thoresby, minister of Spa Fields Chapel: 'I am at last imprisoned—they say for contempt of court, for non-payment of the Bishop's costs—but really and virtually for preaching the Gospel outside the Established Church.' The costs were paid as a result of public subscription, and Shore henceforth safeguarded his position by taking out a licence as a dissenting minister.

The friendship of the Countess of Huntingdon's Connexion and the Free Church of England was strengthened by these tribulations. Thomas Thoresby, an able man with a large and flourishing congregation of his own, drew up a constitution for the new Church. His interest had been stimulated by discovering a draft plan among the papers of the Countess of Huntingdon. It was evident that the Countess had envisaged some sort of free Church of England for her own organisation.

So amicable were the relations of the Free Church of England with the Connexion that, although the new constitution gave recognition to episcopacy, both denominations united under one president. The title 'bishop' was not employed. This formal union lasted only five years, though it appears to have been cordial. The Free Church of England had been recruited from Evangelical Churchmen who were attached to episcopacy, and in 1868 an attempt was made to force the hand of the President, Benjamin Price, on the occasion of his visit to Bury, Lancashire, to consecrate St. John's Church, Tottington. Price was announced as 'bishop primus' of the Free Church of England. That year the union was dissolved, and Benjamin Price, the joint president, became bishop of the Free Church of England alone. It will be understood that at this period no claim was made to valid episcopal orders. Indeed it is today one of the principles of this Church that recognition is given to episcopacy, 'not as of Divine right, but as a very ancient and desirable form of Church polity'. Also at this period Bishop Cummins and other Evangelical leaders in the Protestant Episcopal Church of America were inveighing against the doctrine of Apostolical Succession.

But the traditions of the Church of England were dear to the communicants of the Free Church of England. They desired a valid consecration. The opportunity came from an unexpected quarter. In the year 1873 George David Cummins, assistant Bishop of Kentucky, seceded from the Protestant Episcopal Church to organise a Reformed Episcopal Church. Thereupon, he consecrated bishops. The Reformed Episcopal Church was not long in establishing contacts with the Free Church of England, and only illness prevented Bishop Cummins from visiting England to consecrate Benjamin Price. The actual consecration was made in 1876 at Christ Church, Teddington, Middlesex, by a bishop of the Reformed Episcopal Church, Dr. Edward Cridge. A Cambridge graduate, he had been the Protestant Episcopal Dean of Victoria, B.C. No formal union was effected between the Reformed Episcopal Church of America and the Free Church of England, but the English Church adopted the Declaration of Principles, which the American Church had promulgated.

Meanwhile, fellowship linked these 'Dissenting Churchmen', as they were sometimes called, with men of like mind in the Establishment. In 1876 the group of extreme Evangelicals in the Church of England who formed the Prayer Book Revision Society issued a special edition of the 'Book of Common Prayer Revised' for 'the use of the Free Church of England'. But, although published, the book was never in general use, probably owing to cost of production.

It would seem that after not a few vicissitudes of fortune the Free Church of England was emerging happily from troubles and difficulties in 1876. The claim of the Church to be Episcopal, Liturgical and Evangelical had been substantiated. Benjamin Price, raised to the episcopate by his own followers, had been consecrated. The attempt to provide the faithful with an Evangelically-edited Prayer Book had been more or less successful, and a Declaration of Principles had been accepted without demur. Under these circumstances, progress was considerable, churches were built and congregations founded. But this advance was not permitted to continue without distraction and dissension. The establishment of a comparatively strong and influential Reformed Episcopal Church across the Atlantic introduced a new and somewhat alien influence which was benevolently, but not always judiciously, exercised. Certain members of the Free Church of England became vigorous advocates of union with the American Church. Constitutional difficulties made this impracticable, but Lord Ebury and his friends of the Prayer Book Revision Society took it upon themselves to petition the American General Council not only to establish a branch Church in England, but to consecrate as first bishop the Rev. Huband Gregg, M.D., D.D., late Vicar of East Harborne, near Birmingham. Dr. Gregg sailed for America, and was consecrated bishop at New York on 20th June 1877. In this way the Reformed Episcopal Church in the United Kingdom was inaugurated.

The new bishop was a man of distinction and force of character. He soon showed his independence of the American General Council by editing an English version of the Reformed Prayer Book, faithful to the doctrine, discipline and worship of the American Church, but a nearer approach to the Anglican liturgy. This action caused a division in the Reformed Episcopal Church, Bishop Gregg's section being known as 'The Reformed Church of England'. But the Reformed Episcopal Church in the United Kingdom was reunited at his death, and the General Council of America conceded complete self-government. From this time onwards the Reformed Episcopal Church in the United Kingdom and the Free Church of England drew closer together, and Bishop Gregg's reformed liturgy came into general use. Indeed the bishop's insistence that the liturgy

73

should be more in accord with the Prayer Book of the Church of England met with increasing approval. In 1904 the General Synod of the Reformed Episcopal Church officially adopted Gregg's edition, but with still further approximations to the Anglican liturgy. In 1911 this same edition was approved by the Free Church of England as a manual of devotion. Indeed, it was to be only a question of time before it became the standard book of both Churches and of the United Church. But before this occurred, one more event of some importance intervened.

In 1920, the Lambeth Conference issued a manifesto on Church Union, appealing for the reunion of Christian Churches. The Northern Diocese of the Reformed Episcopal Church was impressed with this declaration, and private negotiations were opened with Anglican bishops. These discussions were not approved by the Southern Diocese which forwarded a resolution to all the bishops of the Church of England, setting forth the conditions of reunion. 'This synod, being desirous, so far as in it lies, of maintaining unity among all Christian people, would be prepared to consider the question of the union of the Reformed Episcopal Church with the Established Church of England, provided that the ministers of the Reformed Episcopal Church are received as clergy duly ordained in accordance with the Thirty-nine Articles of Religion, and that it be allowed to retain its Declaration of Principles unaltered, with its Doctrine, Discipline and Worship, as set forth in its Constitutions and Canons and Prayer Book.' The matter was given consideration by a committee of the Lambeth Conference which declined to accept the claim made as to a valid episcopate, and recommended the conference not to enter into negotiations with the synod.

Although this suggested reunion proved abortive, proposals to unite the Reformed Episcopal Church with the Free Church of England progressed so satisfactorily that in 1927 union was effected. The United Church henceforth was styled, 'The Free Church of England otherwise called the Reformed Episcopal Church'. The United Church remained true to its claims to be Episcopal, Evangelical and Liturgical. A bishop primus was appointed, the Declaration of Principles accepted as fundamental doctrine, and the edition of the Prayer Book of 1904 approved as the standard book.

The history of this Church is largely the story of prayer-book reform, and of a determined attempt on the part of uncompromising Evangelicals to purge the Prayer Book of all those elements that made sacerdotalism, ritualism, and Anglo-Catholicism possible. For, as Dr. Pusey wrote to Dr. Gregg in 1882, 'the Tractarians of 1833 and onward learned their belief through the Church of England in her Prayer Book, and consequently, while the Prayer Book remains untouched, Tractarianism cannot be shaken.'

The resolute attempt of liturgical reformers in England and America to provide Evangelicals with a Prayer Book completely at one with the Holy Scriptures is an interesting and impressive phase of spiritual life during the last two centuries. Because their loyalty to Evangelical principles proved stronger than their allegiance to the ancient Church of England, these enthusiasts brought forth not only reformed prayer books, but new religious communions.

Regarded simply as a sect, the Free Church of England is not of first-rate importance. Numerically it remains one of the lesser groups of Christendom. But this is to misunderstand the real significance of this movement. The creation of new Evangelical Churches by English and American churchmen in the nineteenth century is an important episode in a struggle for prayer-book revision that has been a continuous feature of religious life since the sixteenth century.

The Free Church of England is the proud heir to three hundred years of Protestant Anglicanism. With some reason it continues to decry any charge of Dissent. In 1936 Dr. Vaughan, the bishop primus, reprinted in his history the words of Bishop Eldridge of the Reformed Episcopal Church. 'If a Dissenter be one who disagrees with the government, doctrine, and worship of the National Church, then we are not Dissenters. We believe in Episcopacy, and possess the historic Episcopate. We believe in the doctrines, and conform to the worship of the Church of England, as set forth and evangelically interpreted in her authorised formularies.'

The standard *Book of Common Prayer for use in the Free Church of England* was adopted by the United Church in 1927. The liturgy has a long ancestry. It is based, with some amendments, on Bishop Gregg's revision of 1879, *The Book of Common Prayer*

of the Reformed Episcopal Church in the United Kingdom. This
revision was derived from the 1662 Book of Common Prayer
of the Church of England, and the 1874 Book of Common
Prayer of the Reformed Episcopal Church of America. It will
be recalled that Dr. Gregg was an ex-Anglican vicar, conse-
crated bishop by the American Reformed Episcopal Church.
Hence the mixed English and American elements in his book.
But the Book of Common Prayer of the Reformed Episcopal
Church of America was itself derived from the 1785 'Proposed
Prayer Book' of America. In the preface to the revised Prayer
Book of the American Reformed Episcopal Church explicit
reference is made to the 'Proposed Book' of 1785, 'upon which
this revision is chiefly based'. In its turn the preface of the
'Proposed Book' refers to the Royal Commission of 1689, 'than
whom (it hath been truly acknowledged) the Church of England
was never, at any one time, blessed with either wiser or better,
since it was a church'. Thus the Prayer Book in use today in
the Free Church of England is based on reforms advocated by
English Puritans and Presbyterians.

The pre-union Free Church of England came into being in
1844, some years before the foundation of the Reformed Episcopal Church of America. It was always essentially an English
Church. From the beginning it attracted men antagonistic to
the Oxford Movement. Thus the Free Church of England
came to be regarded as a bulwark against Anglo-Catholicism,
and as such won the approval of Lord Ebury and the Prayer
Book Revision Society. Until the adoption of Bishop Gregg's
Reformed Episcopal Prayer Book in 1911, it was the practice
of this Church to utilise an incomplete liturgy with many
services omitted, viz. *The Book of Common Prayer Revised according
to the use of the Free Church of England* (1876). This book was not
in use in the Reformed Episcopal Church.

The Reformed Episcopal Church in the United Kingdom
was founded in 1877 at a time when the Oxford Movement had
blossomed into a powerful Anglo-Catholicism. The Reformed
Episcopal Church, despite its nomenclature, was a thoroughly
English institution. It was at one with the Free Church of
England in offering uncompromising opposition to ritualism
and Anglo-Catholicism.

This resistance was embodied in a Declaration of Principles,

first adopted by the Reformed Episcopal Church of America in
1873. It was accepted by the Free Church of England in 1876,
and by the English Reformed Episcopal Church. The Declaration is still authoritative teaching and is incorporated in the
present Standard Book of the Free Church of England. It
avows fidelity to 'the faith once delivered unto the Saints' and
proclaims the Holy Scriptures of the Old and New Testaments
as the Word of God and the sole rule of faith and practice.
Adherence is declared to the creed, 'commonly called the
Apostles' Creed', to the divine institution of the sacraments of
Baptism and the Lord's Supper, and to the doctrines of grace
substantially as they are set forth in the Thirty-nine articles of
religion. Recognition is given to episcopacy, 'not as of Divine
right, but as a very ancient and desirable form of Church
polity'. The use of a liturgy is retained but this 'shall not be
repressive of freedom of prayer', and the Book of Common
Prayer is accepted, 'as it was revised, prepared, and recommended for use by the General Convention of the Protestant
Episcopal Church A.D. 1785, reserving full liberty to alter,
abridge, enlarge, and amend the same, as may seem most
conducive to the edification of the people, "provided that the
substance of the faith be kept entire" '.

The Declaration proceeds to denounce particular tenets
of Catholic teaching. 'This Church condemns and rejects
the following erroneous and strange doctrines as contrary to
God's Word. First, that the Church of Christ exists only in one
order or form of ecclesiastical polity. Second, that Christian
ministers are "priests" in another sense than that in which all
believers are "a royal priesthood". Third, that the Lord's Table
is an altar on which the oblation of the Body and Blood of
Christ is offered anew to the Father; Fourth, that the presence
of Christ in the Lord's Supper is a presence in the elements of
Bread and Wine; Fifth, that regeneration is inseparably connected with baptism.'

The Free Church of England remains adamant to Anglo-
Catholicism. 'We must be', said Bishop Rudolf of the Reformed
Episcopal Church, 'the Protestants of the Protestants.' It is
curious to observe that the last chapter to be considered in this
section is as much concerned with Anglo-Catholicism as with
Roman Catholicism. Indeed rather more so, for the Anglo-

Catholics now appear as the more immediate adversaries. It was the Gorham Case (1847) that raised the whole issue of baptismal regeneration, and by a strange irony the principal participant on the High Church side was once again Dr. Phillpotts. It was he who challenged George Cornelius Gorham, Fellow of Queen's College, Cambridge, as previously he had challenged James Shore.

At first the issue between the Evangelicals and the Tractarians centred on the nature of baptism. But on the 14th May 1843, Dr. Pusey preached a famous sermon at Christ Church, Oxford, on the theme of the 'Holy Eucharist a Comfort to the Penitent'. Pusey affirmed the doctrines of the Real Presence in the consecrated elements, and the Eucharistic Sacrifice. Henceforth the nature of the Eucharist became increasingly the issue in the Church of England. In 1859 an association was formed by the extreme Evangelicals, under the leadership of Lord Ebury, 'for promoting a revision of the Prayer Book, and a review of the Acts of Uniformity'. Ebury perceived that the real problem of the Evangelicals was the doctrine sanctioned or permitted by the occasional services. It was true that these services were not in frequent use. But they were an inherent part of the Prayer Book, and gave countenance to those Catholic practices most detested by him, auricular confession and priestly absolution. Ebury met with almost complete failure. Only in the Free Church of England, free of State authority, was it possible to legislate against vestments, and to remove obnoxious words from 'The Ordering of Priests', 'Whose sins thou dost forgive, they are forgiven', and from 'The Visitation of the Sick', 'I absolve thee from all thy sins'.

Leaders of the Free Church of England have never ceased to entertain the hope that dissatisfied Evangelicals in the Church of England would unite with them. Bishop Vaughan in his *History* quotes Bishop Eldridge. 'Our aim is to provide an ecclesiastical and spiritual home for those Church-people who, on account of what is popularly called "Ritualism", can no longer find such a home in the Church of their fathers.' But the response of Evangelicals in the Church of England has not been encouraging.

It is not to be expected that theological developments will

be found in the prayer books of this Church. The Bible and the Bible only remains the norm of Free Evangelical Anglicanism. That is why, of late years, not only Catholicism but Modernism has been denounced and repudiated. This is made clear in an address by Bishop Rudolf entitled, 'The Mission of Our Church'. 'If, on the one hand, the Church of Jesus Christ is under obligation to oppose Romanism, on the other she must as faithfully set her face against the proud and destructive claims of Rationalism. . . . There is undoubtedly a drift in Protestantism, so called, towards a doctrine of salvation on the ground of the merit of good works. It is associated with the relinquishment of the doctrine of the infallibility of the Scriptures, the doctrine of the essential Deity of Christ, and the doctrine of eternal punishment.' No compromise with Modernism is tolerated by Bishop Rudolf's Church. Sunday school teachers are cautioned in Part I of *The Teachers' Catechism*, 'to guard against the Modernist error known as the Universal Fatherhood of God, which declares that all are by nature the children of God, thus denying by implication, if not by direct assertion, the necessity of the New Birth, by which alone we become the children of God and He becomes our Father'.

As for the theory of evolution, it is repudiated. Reference is made in *The Teachers' Catechism* to the creation story of Genesis. 'Many learned men have tried to prove that this first chapter of the Bible is not true, but only "a sort of beautiful, poetic fairy-tale or legend". They say that the world and everything in it, gradually evolved or unfolded itself out, from a little speck to what it is now! What are we to believe, the Bible or the so-called scientists?'

The unalterable position of the Free Church of England is summed up by G. Hugh Jones in his article, 'The Free Church of England, its doctrines and ecclesiastical polity', published in 1916. 'The Free Church of England has not a new message to attract and fascinate the unstable. It is that of the Apostles, and strictly according to the Scriptures. The testimony of the early Fathers and the customs of the post-apostolic or mediaeval periods must not influence either mind or conscience. The Holy Scriptures are its sole guide and final court of appeal.'

The various prayer books of the Free Church of England and the Reformed Episcopal Church differ, but only in minor

79

detail. An examination of the 'Standard Book', adopted by the United Church in 1927, and still in use presents the salient features of all these liturgies.

· It will be observed that true to all Puritan and Evangelical amendments revisions are effected almost invariably by way of omissions, and not by additions. Catholic rites and doctrines are pruned away. In all places the word 'Priest' is changed to 'Minister', or 'Presbyter'. Apocryphal lessons are excluded. Collects for Saints' Days are removed. The words, "Mattins" and "Evensong", are not used.

An Examination of the Standard Book
Rites and Ceremonies

There are stringent regulations as to the use of vestments. 'The Minister at the time of the holy Communion, and at all other times in his public Ministration of the Services of the Church, shall use neither Alb, Vestment, nor Cope, but being a Bishop he shall have and wear a Rochet and Chimere; and being a Presbyter or Deacon he shall have and wear a plain Surplice and a plain black scarf, with or without the Hood pertaining to his degree. A black gown may be worn in the pulpit.' It will be noted that these regulations are similar to those stipulated by the Second Prayer Book of Edward VI (1552), though discarded under Elizabeth. Candles, incense, cross, and crucifix are forbidden.

Table of Lessons

Lessons from the Apocrypha are expunged.

Morning Prayer

This service is shortened. 'It shall not be necessary to repeat any Prayer or Collect which has once been used during the same Service, or to use more than one Creed, or one Form of Prayer for the King's Majesty, when various services are combined.' On the other hand, 'A short extemporaneous Prayer may be used before and after the Sermon, or upon emergent occasions.'

THE ABSOLUTION

The words, 'The Absolution, or Remission of sins' are changed to 'The Declaration concerning the Remission of sins'. The words, 'and hath given power, and commandment, to his Ministers, to declare and pronounce to his people, being penitent, the Absolution and Remission of their sins', are bracketed. They may be omitted, or if used, understood only in the sense of 2 Cor. v, 18–21. The word 'Priest' is changed here, as elsewhere, to 'Minister'.

BENEDICITE

The verses, 'O ye Priests of the Lord', and 'O Ananias, Azarias, and Misael', are omitted.

QUICUNQUE VULT

The 'Damnatory' clauses are removed.

THE LITANY

The word 'deadly' is placed in brackets. The Presbyterians at the Savoy Conference had suggested 'heinous' or 'grievous'. They had distrusted the Roman Catholic distinction between mortal and venial sins. The 1689 Commission omitted 'deadly sin'.

SAINTS' DAYS

All collects for Saints' Days are omitted.

Holy Communion

A rubric forbids the placing of candle or cross on the Lord's Table, 'nor shall the colour of its covering be changed to indicate the Church seasons'.

The minister is forbidden to kneel or pray, 'with his back to the people in the Body of the Church'.

OFFERTORY SERVICES

Tobit iv, 7, 8 and 9 are removed.

PRAYER FOR WHOLE STATE OF CHRIST'S CHURCH

The word 'oblations' is removed.

FIRST EXHORTATION

Very much shortened. The 'most comfortable sacrament of the Body and Blood of Christ', is changed to the 'most comfortable sacrament of the Lord's Supper'.

THIRD EXHORTATION

The words 'holy mysteries' are changed to 'holy supper'.
N.B. Ministers are authorised to invite 'Fellow Christians of other branches of Christ's Church' to the Lord's Table.

ABSOLUTION

The term 'Absolution' is omitted.

PRAYER OF HUMBLE ACCESS

The prayer is changed to read, 'Grant us therefore, gracious Lord, so spiritually to eat the flesh of thy dear Son.'

PRAYER OF CONSECRATION

The manual acts are included. The words 'after an heavenly and spiritual manner' are inserted before the words, 'be partakers of his most blessed Body and Blood'.
N.B. Reservation of the sacrament is prohibited.

Public Baptism of Infants

A rubric declares that 'every child to be baptised shall be presented by the Parents or Guardians, and such other fit persons as they shall choose to be associated with them as Sponsors'.

The words, 'it is certain by God's word, that children which are baptised, dying before they commit actual sin, are undoubtedly saved', are omitted.

All references to the doctrine of baptismal regeneration are deleted. The Exhortation is abridged, and the words 'born anew of water' removed.

THE FIRST PRAYER

This is omitted. The Presbyterian Divines at the Savoy expressed their dislike of the notion of the sanctification of Jordan, or any other waters, to a sacramental use by the baptism of Christ.

THE SECOND PRAYER

The words 'that he, coming to thy Holy Baptism, may receive remission of his sins by spiritual regeneration', are omitted.

EXHORTATION ON THE GOSPEL

The words, 'Doubt ye not therefore . . . that he will give unto him the blessing of eternal life, and make him partaker of his everlasting Kingdom', are removed.

THE ADDRESS TO SPONSORS

The vicarious stipulations are removed. The sponsors promise to instruct the child.

SANCTIFICATION OF THE WATER

The words, 'sanctify this water to the mystical washing away of sin', are deleted.

D

THE RECEPTION, AND SIGN OF THE CROSS

The reception remains, but the sign of the cross, and the words pertaining thereto, are removed.

THE EXHORTATION TO THANKSGIVING

The words, 'this child is regenerate', are deleted. The sentence becomes, 'grafted into the body of Christ's visible Church'.

THE THANKSGIVING PRAYER

This prayer is altered. It begins, 'We yield thee hearty thanks, most merciful Father, that it hath pleased thee to incline us to dedicate this child to thee in Baptism.' N.B. The child is to be confirmed when attaining 'years of discretion'.

Private Baptism

This office is included, with similar changes.

Baptism to such as are of Riper Years

The changes are similar. But the sign of the cross is optional.
N.B. The teaching of the Free Church of England as to Baptism is summarised in their *Teachers' Catechism*, Part I. 'Baptism does not put us into the second Church, the spiritual Body of Christ of all born again. If it did, then Baptism would make us Christians, which it never does and cannot do. But Baptism does give us a place in the prayers and interests and benefits of the Christian congregation, the Visible Church.'

Confirmation

The Free Church of England retains the Order of Confirmation as an Apostolic custom, but new members from other Churches need not be confirmed, except at their own desire.
References to baptismal regeneration are expunged. The candidate is called upon solemnly to profess repentance towards God, and faith towards our Lord Jesus Christ.

84

Holy Matrimony

The Address is abridged. The ring is used, but the words, 'with my body I thee worship' are expunged.

Visitation of the Sick

The Free Church of England does not countenance auricular confession or priestly absolution, and the rubric, 'Here shall the sick person be moved to make a special confession of his sins' is left out. So is the Absolution with the words, 'I absolve thee from all thy sins'.

Communion of the Sick

This service is not changed.

Burial of the Dead

THE COMMENDATION

The words in the commendation, 'to take unto himself the soul of our dear brother here departed' are changed to 'take out of this world the soul of our dear brother here departed'. The Presbyterians at the Savoy had argued that the words in the Prayer Book 'cannot in truth be said of persons living and dying in open and notorious sins'.

THE PRAYER, 'ALMIGHTY GOD'

The sentence, 'We give thee hearty thanks, for that it hath pleased thee to deliver this our brother out of the miseries of this sinful world', is removed, and replaced by, 'We give thee hearty thanks for all thy servants departed this life in thy faith and fear.'

Churching of Women

This service is not changed.

A Commination

A Penitential Service is substituted for the Commination Service and is based upon it. But the comminations are removed.

The Ordinal

The Free Church of England is prepared to receive into her ministry Evangelical ministers of other denominations without Episcopal ordination. A form is included in the Ordinal, 'of receiving a Presbyter of another church'. In the preface, 'Priest' is changed to 'Presbyter', and the word 'Episcopal' is omitted from the sentence, 'No man shall be accounted or taken to be a lawful Bishop, Priest, or Deacon . . . except he be called, tried, examined, and admitted thereunto, according to the form hereafter following, or hath had formerly Episcopal consecration or ordination.'

The Ordering of Deacons

The service closely follows the Prayer Book. The Bishop lays hands on the ordinand, and gives him the 'Holy Scriptures'.

The Ordering of Presbyters

This service closely follows the Prayer Book. The Bishop and Presbyters present lay on hands.

'RECEIVE THE HOLY GHOST'

This is replaced by a petition to God for the gift of the Holy Ghost. It begins, 'Almighty God grant unto thee the gift of the Holy Ghost for the office and work of a Presbyter in the Church of God, now committed unto thee by the imposition of our hands.' The words, 'Whose sins thou dost forgive, they are forgiven' etc., are removed. It is to be remembered that the Royal Commission of 1689 advocated a similar though not identical change, 'Whereas it was the constant practice of the Church to ordain by prayer, which practice continued for many ages, and that the pronouncing these words, "Receive the Holy Ghost", in the imperative mood, was brought into the Office of Ordination in the darkest times of popery.'

The Consecration of Bishops

This service closely follows the Prayer Book. The Bishops present, with three or more Presbyters, lay on hands.

The lesson from St. John xx, which contains the words of absolution (verse 23) is omitted.

'RECEIVE THE HOLY GHOST'

This is replaced by a petition to God for the gift of the Holy Ghost.

The words, 'by this imposition of our hands' are omitted.

Articles of Religion

These are almost identical with the Articles of the Church of England. But Article VI expressly disavows the Apocrypha. Article XVI is changed from 'Sin after Baptism' to 'Sin after Conversion'. Article XXVIII includes a repudiation of consubstantiation. An Article forbidding Auricular Confession replaces Article XXXIII, and an Article repudiating 'Apostolic Succession' replaces Article XXXV.

GENEALOGICAL TABLE OF THE PRESENT 'STANDARD BOOK' OF THE FREE CHURCH OF ENGLAND, OTHERWISE CALLED THE REFORMED EPISCOPAL CHURCH IN THE UNITED KINGDOM

Presbyterian Reforms suggested at Savoy Conference, 1661.

Book of Common Prayer as amended by Royal Commission, 1689.

Proposed Prayer Book of America, 1785.

Book of Common Prayer of Reformed = Book of Common Prayer of Episcopal Church of America, 1874.   Church of England, 1662.

Book of Common Prayer | Book of Common Prayer revised for use of Free revised according to use of Church of England, 1876. Free Church of England, (Prayer Book Revision 1876. Society).

Book of Common Prayer of Reformed Episcopal Church in United Kingdom, 1879 (Bishop Gregg's Revision).

The 'Standard Book'.
Adopted by Reformed Episcopal Church, 1904.
Adopted by Free Church of England, 1911.
Adopted by United Church, 1927.

PART II

The Dissenting Tradition

In this, the second part of the book, another group of liturgies calls for examination. They are the liturgies of the Moravians, the Congregationalists, the Baptists, and Churches of Christ. As may be expected the prayer books of these denominations are not in the Anglican tradition, though influenced by it. The Methodists, Lady Huntingdon's Connexion, and the Free Church of England are the offsprings of the Church of England, and proud of their parentage. But the denominations, whose liturgies are now under review, have a very different heritage. The *Unitas Fratrum*, or Moravian Church, emerged at Lititz in Bohemia in 1457. It was not until the middle of the eighteenth century that it came to be established in England. The Congregationalists are the historic Independents, with origins going back to the days of Mary and the first Elizabeth. The ancestors of Congregationalists and Baptists alike refused to acquiesce in the Elizabethan settlement. Very different are the origins of Churches of Christ which are to be found in eighteenth-century Scotland.

These Free Churches have long traditions of their own. They are reflected in their attitude to liturgical worship.

CHAPTER VI

THE MORAVIANS

JOHN HUS was elected Rector of the University of Prague in 1402. There was a singular commonalty of learning in mediaeval Christendom, and friendly relations existed between the University of Prague and the University of Oxford. The wandering scholars of the period passed easily between them. Social and academic fellowship was fostered by a royal wedding. It is known that following the marriage of Richard II to his beloved Anne of Bohemia copies of John Wycliffe's works found their way to her native land. The consequences were far reaching. Hus developed an enthusiasm for the great Oxford Schoolman. The Hussite Movement swept Bohemia. There was betrayal and martyrdom, and Hus became the hero of his nation. Hussite and Catholic Leagues were formed, and the Hussite Wars began. But the Hussites were divided. The conservative wing was composed of Utraquists or Calixtines, who emblazoned the Cup on their banners. They contended that the laity should be permitted to take the wine at Communion, a doctrine taught by Hus in his later years. The radical wing was formed of several groups. Such were the Taborites, with Socialist ideas of property, and the Waldenses, who cherished ideals of a primitive Christianity. In 1433 the Utraquists came to terms with the papacy, their practices being recognised by Rome. In Bohemia, the laity were permitted Communion in both kinds. The Taborites thus deserted were crushed in battle. It was amid this desolation that the Moravian Church came into being.

Resolute to preserve the spiritual teaching of Hus, and disgusted with the prevailing anarchy in the State, a group of people gathered round a former monk named Gregory. This Gregory, often called the Patriarch, had been attracted by the writings of Peter of Chelcic, a Bohemian Tolstoy. Gregory's uncle, Rockycana, Archbishop-elect of Prague, persuaded the king to permit this group to settle in Kunwald, a secluded village in the north-east of Bohemia. Here they took the Bible for their law, and Christ for their King. At the Synod of Lhota (1467) they separated from Rome, and elected ministers by lot. Their priest, Michael Bradacius, was raised to the episcopate, and consecrated by a Waldensian bishop. Henceforth the Brethren became, what they remain, a Protestant Episcopal Church.

In spite of sporadic persecution the Church grew, many of the scholars and nobility of Bohemia being attracted by its strict discipline and emphasis on conduct rather than creed. Under the influence of Bishop Luke of Prague, learning was fostered. It has been computed that in the early sixteenth century, the Brethren published five-sixths of the works printed in Bohemia. In 1501 they published the first Church hymnal. Towards the end of the century they issued a Bohemian version of the Bible, the first to be translated, not from the Vulgate, but from the original Hebrew and Greek. This version has been to the Czech language what the Authorised Version is to the English. It won the praise even of the Jesuits and is still published by the British and Foreign Bible Society.

It is sober truth to say that the history of the *Unitas Fratrum* reads like a saga. After a golden age, almost contemporaneous with the Elizabethan era, the Brethren drank deep of their Master's bitter cup. In 1609 they numbered half the Protestants in Bohemia, and more than half in Moravia. In 1620, after the defeat of Frederick the 'Winter King', they were exposed to one of the bitterest persecutions in history. Word was sent to the pope that the Church of the Brethren was no more.

Complete extinction was averted by the genius of Bishop Comenius, the 'Father of the Elementary School', and writer of the allegory, 'The Labyrinth of the World and the Paradise of the Heart'. Comenius cherished the 'Hidden Seed' of the Faithful, still worshipping in Moravia and Poland. This stoical fidelity was admired in England. Cromwell offered the Brethren a home in Ireland. Anglican dignitaries assisted with money. 'To you, dear friends', wrote Comenius to them, 'we commit our dear mother, the Church herself. Even in her death, which seems approaching, you ought to love her.'

But the Church was not to die. Some German-speaking stalwarts survived in the neighbourhood of Fulneck in Moravia. (Hence the prevalent name Moravian.) Persecuted with relentless cruelty, these poor people were rescued by the enterprise and intrepid daring of a carpenter, Christian David, a convert from Rome. He it was who found them sanctuary in Lutheran Saxony, and led them forth to Count Zinzendorf's estate at Herrnhut. Zinzendorf was a fervent Lutheran of the Pietist type. In his well-ordered Pietist community the Moravians attended at first the Lutheran parish church. Zinzendorf saw in them ideal material for his plans of world-wide Evangelism. The spiritual life of the community was intense, expressing itself in new forms of worship, new expressions of congregational life, and above all in new enterprises for the spread of the gospel. From Herrnhut went out in 1732 the first foreign missionaries, 'the advance guard of the modern missionary movement'. At first Zinzendorf tried to confine the spiritual life of his community to the Lutheran Church, but that Church was too narrow for his own imaginative, sympathetic, and tolerant religious genius. Eventually, the combination of Zinzendorf's enthusiasm and the practical zeal of the Moravian exiles formed a new ecclesiastical organisation which both parties recognised as the renewal of the old *Unitas Fratrum*. In this Church Zinzendorf received the episcopate from the hands of the grandson of Comenius. The 'Hidden Seed' had at last come to fruit. A special Communion service at Berthelsdorf, on 13th August 1727, had such a unifying experience that modern Moravians regard it as the birthday of the renewed Church. The old title of *Unitas Fratrum* was restored.

It was because Zinzendorf's settlements attracted more refugees than could be accommodated that the Count conceived the idea of sending colonists to North America. Thus he despatched a few Moravians to establish colonies in Pennsylvania and Georgia. Far-reaching repercussions ensued. On his voyage to Georgia in 1735, John Wesley met some Moravian emigrants. Later he encountered Peter Boehler in London. Boehler was a scholar and a gentleman. It was through his influence that John and his brother Charles were converted.

But Zinzendorf's influence was not altogether happy for his co-religionists. He was a great man, but the vagaries of his

93

genius had distressing consequences. He was at heart a poet. His hymn, 'Jesus, still lead on', is as beloved in Germany as is 'Abide with me', in England. But the poet is seldom a statesman. For many years Zinzendorf's pietism checked the Moravian advance. His policy of maintaining settlements on the estates of friendly noblemen led to stagnation. His evangelising of the 'diaspora' in the German State Churches impeded denominational growth, though Schleiermacher never forgot how much he owed to this influence. It was lamentable that the renewed Church of the Brethren was so much at the mercy of this godly, rich Count-Bishop.

It was due to Zinzendorf's desire to secure the goodwill of English Churchmen for his North American colonists that the Moravians first came to England. In 1737 Zinzendorf arrived in London for a short visit. He consulted the secretary of the Board of Trustees for Georgia. The secretary was Charles Wesley. Charles introduced the Count to James Hutton, the son of a High Church clergyman. This London bookseller was destined to become the first English member of the Brethren's Church. Also he was the connecting link between the Moravians and the Methodists. It was at a religious society founded by Hutton in Aldersgate Street that John Wesley was converted. This society was composed almost entirely of Anglicans, and was not a Moravian society as is sometimes assumed. The society increased, and a hall was hired in Fetter Lane. Hutton and Charles Wesley were here the leading spirits. John Wesley visited Herrnhut in 1738, but took an angry departure from the Fetter Lane society in 1740. It was due to Hutton that the society became increasingly Moravian in character. It was he who published a collection of Moravian hymns and a volume in English of Zinzendorf's discourses. From the membership of the Fetter Lane society the first London congregation of the Brethren was drawn in 1742.

In 1749 the *Unitas Fratrum* was recognised by the British Parliament as 'an ancient protestant episcopal church'. But it was not until 1853 that the English Moravians decided to promote 'the extension of the Brethren's Church'. This delay was a legacy of the 'diaspora' policy and settlement system. The traveller today, who encounters the peaceful and picturesque settlements of Fulneck near Leeds, Ockbrook near Derby, or

Fairfield near Manchester, cannot fail to be charmed with these eighteenth-century hamlets, complete with church, manse, houses for brethren and sisters and excellent boarding-schools. But a retreat is not an ideal centre for an expanding Church. The settlement system, imported to England from Germany, was a doubtful blessing. So was the extreme policy of centralisation. New churches blossomed, only to wither and die. Converts were not encouraged. The 'diaspora' policy was as fatal in Britain as in Germany. Zinzendorf arrived in England in 1746 enthused with a scheme to incorporate the Moravian churches within the Church of England. His ministers were to be ordained by both Anglican and Moravian bishops. His Brethren were to use the Prayer Book. To his great surprise, he encountered opposition. The Archbishop of Canterbury would not hear of it. But ideas survive. Zinzendorf's 'Tropus Idea' may yet be a contribution to Christian unity. The Count believed that over and above all the Christian Churches was one ideal universal Christian Church representing the original religion of Christ. He considered that the true mission of the Brethren was to make this ideal Church a reality upon earth. He regarded the Lutheran, Calvinist, Moravian and other so-called churches as 'tropuses' or religious schools for the training of Christians for membership in the one true Church of Christ. He hoped that his broad, comprehensive 'Church of the Brethren' would come to include men from every tropus.

Meanwhile the well-meaning Brethren were meeting ignorant and scurrilous abuse. John Wesley and Whitefield joined the attack. It appears they had been persuaded that the Brethren were guilty of antinomianism. This atrocious libel was refuted by the Sunday morning Litany. So far from despising good works, these kindly hearted people were reciting:

O, that we might never see a necessitous person go unrelieved.
O, that we might be eyes to the blind and feet to the lame.
Yea, may our hearts rejoice to see it go well with our enemies.

The truth would seem to be that the Count was not always prudent and precise in his theological expositions. An increasing reliance upon the Biblical practice of casting Lots was vitiating his judgment. Repelled by the cold rationalism of the Lutheran Church, Zinzendorf enunciated a famous 'Blood and Wounds' Theology, and composed a 'Litany of the Wounds of Jesus' (1743). It is true that at first he stressed the moral and spiritual value of the cross. But later he dwelt on meticulous physical details as in this Litany. The German Brethren expressed their devotion in language that was not restrained. Soon they awoke to their error. But exaggerated and distorted rumours of these things did their Brethren in England much harm. It is pleasing to record that later in life John Wesley resumed friendly relations with his old Moravian colleagues.

The first London congregation was established at Fetter Lane in 1742. For many years this church remained the headquarters of Moravian work in Great Britain. Here was held the first 'watch-night' service in England. During the nineteenth century the Moravians became well known for their boarding-schools. A high moral tone has made them acceptable to the parents of all denominations. Gradually the English branch of the Church lost the old German characteristics. Today, the international Church is supervised by a General Synod, Great Britain constituting a self-governing province. Many years ago the use of the Lot was discontinued. Modern Brethren seek their Lord's guidance, not in any mechanical way, but through prayer. The older congregations still retain the Love-feasts, regular choir festivals, and Memorial Days. But to some of the new congregations these are unknown.

Moravians refute the charge of Dissent. They are members of a Protestant Episcopal Church. In this respect their position is not unlike that of the Free Church of England, and it is interesting to recall that a Moravian bishop assisted at the consecration of a Free Church of England bishop in 1921. But the Moravians exchange pulpits with Nonconformists, and admit to Communion members of all Evangelical denominations. For they still claim to be a Union Church. 'Perish sects', cried Bishop Comenius, in the seventeenth century. Today they advocate reunion on a broad Scriptural basis. In so doing they remain true to the dearest wish of Zinzendorf.

The crowning glory of Moravian achievement has been the mission field. 'See what these Moravians have done', exclaimed

William Carey. Zinzendorf taught the Brethren that their chief task was 'to proclaim the Saviour to the World'. Hence the Moravians were the first Protestants to declare the evangelising of the heathen to be the duty of the Church. In 1732 their missionaries arrived in the West Indies. It was there that the parents of James Montgomery sickened and died. Their son proclaimed the reign of Christ in his hymn, 'Hail to the Lord's Anointed'. The story that these missionaries became slaves is legend. But they worked as the slaves of Christ among the slaves.

The modern Moravians remain true to their general principle that Holy Scripture alone is the standard of faith. They have a respect for the historic creeds, but decline to enforce subscription. Of candidates for Church membership one thing only is asked. 'Do you believe in Jesus Christ who loved you and gave Himself for you?' Of ministers, at ordination, one doctrinal assurance only is sought. 'Do you accept the Holy Scriptures, and above all, the living Word, Jesus Christ our Lord, as giving the true revelation of God, and His will towards men?" These words encircle their ancient episcopal seal: *Vicit Agnus noster: Eum sequamur.* It is still their faith.

THE MORAVIANS AND THEIR WORSHIP

A remarkable tolerance of mind exists in this Protestant Episcopal Church. Episcopal ordination is the rule, and only bishops may ordain. But Protestant ministers not episcopally ordained have been received into this ministry. Holy Communion is celebrated normally on the first Sunday in the month, on Maundy Thursday, Easter Day, at Synod and on other special occasions, but the celebrant may be presbyter or deacon. The numerous Communion hymns in the hymn book are derived from all sections of the Christian Church. Some Moravians may believe in the Real Presence, but others do not. The Church does not define the precise meaning of the rite, and ordinary bread or wafer may be used. Infant Baptism is observed, but baptismal regeneration is not an article of Faith. The three modes of admission to full communicant membership are Adult Baptism, Confirmation and Reception. But

Confirmation is administered as a rule by the resident minister, and is not always demanded. The Church Year is observed, but is not held to be obligatory. With such a freedom of belief and practice it is not surprising that the Moravians have never despaired of the unity of Christendom.

Regular Sunday morning worship consists of liturgy, Scripture lessons, preaching, singing and extemporary prayer. Some congregations do not use the liturgy at Sunday evening service. The rubric reads: 'A liturgic form of prayer is used at one Public Service at least on each Lord's Day.' No rules about vestments exist. But it is customary for the clergy to wear the surplice at the Holy Communion, Baptisms, Confirmations, Ordinations and Weddings.

The *Unitas Fratrum* was the first Church to issue a Hymn Book in the language of the people (1501). Thus the Bohemian Brethren were the founders of congregational singing. The first three editions were in Bohemian, and were edited by Luke of Prague (1501, 1505, 1519). The first edition had only eighty-four hymns, but the tenth, 743. Later editions were published in Bohemian, German and Polish. Among the tunes were Gregorian Chants and the popular rondels of the day. At first the *Unitas Fratrum* had no prescribed Order of Worship. But in 1566 Luther's Litany was added to the Hymn Book.

At Herrnhut, in the early days of the Renewed Church, Luther's hymns and Litany were used. This was because the settlers were within the parish of Berthelsdorf and attended the parish church. There are indications, however, that with the growth of the community, and the gradual separation from Berthelsdorf, the leadership of worship in the settlement was assumed increasingly by Zinzendorf. It is known that hymns selected or composed by him were in use at Herrnhut before 1730. Between 1725 and 1731 Zinzendorf published no less than four hymn books.

In 1735 the first official collection of hymns for the Herrnhut community was issued, *Das Gesang-Buch der Gemeine in Herrn-huth*. It consisted chiefly of Brethren's hymns, many being the work of Zinzendorf. During the next fifteen years this book was much enlarged, but with hymns of an indifferent standard. It remained in use until the great collection of more than 3,000 hymns, known as *Das Londoner Gesangbuch*, appeared in two parts, during 1753-4. In 1778 a new collection was published by the distinguished hymnologist Christian Gregor.

Along with the hymns mentioned above the Herrnhut community used a slightly modified form of the 1529 version of Luther's Litany. This was printed in the Brethren's Hymn Book of 1566, and continued to be used until 1741. But their spiritual experience soon demanded something more positive than this Litany. Leonard Dober, who was for some years Chief Elder of the whole Church, was commissioned to prepare a Form of Worship which should give expression to the new life of the Brethren. In this task he was assisted by Zinzendorf.

Thus the first Moravian version of the Litany appeared in 1742 in the 11th Appendix to the hymn book. In 1744 the first German 'Liturgy Book' of the Renewed Church was issued by Zinzendorf. The Litany of 1742 was inserted with slight amendments.

The Moravian version was something more than a revision of Luther's Litany. It departed from the old conceptions of a Litany in three ways.

In the first place the character of the Litany was changed. A note of confidence and joy replaced the sombre tones. The deprecations were directed against spiritual as well as material evils. The passages relating to the life, sufferings, and death of Christ were amplified. The life of the Church was treated with greater fullness. And the topic of Christian missions to the heathen was introduced. This would appear to mark the first appearance of this theme in the public prayers of the Christian Church. As such it is of high interest and significance. The world of the eighteenth-century European was expanding. England and France were engaged in a titanic Seven Years' War for enormous territories in America and Asia. Captain Cook was making historic voyages in the southern hemisphere. In India English nabobs were amassing fabulous fortunes. It is true that Voltaire's Chinaman was astonished at a *Universal History* that could ignore China. But the *Conversation with a Chinese* was itself evidence of a changing outlook. Cultured Europeans were becoming world conscious. Times were propitious for Christians to teach all nations. And in this work the Moravians were pioneers. It is true that prayers for the pagans had been said at Mass in the Roman Church for very many centuries. But it was not until the nineteenth century that a Mass for the pagans, *Missa pro propagatione fidei*, was introduced by Gregory XVI. The Church of England prays for 'Jews, Turks, Infidels, and Hereticks' in the third collect for Good Friday. But no prayer for Missions has been included, as yet, in her Prayer Book.

It may be noted, however, that two prayers 'For Christian Missions Abroad' were added to the Prayer Book of the Church of Ireland in 1878. A thanksgiving 'For Foreign Missions' was added in 1926, and 'A Prayer for Christian Missions' included in 'A Form of Thanksgiving for the Blessings of the Harvest'. A prayer 'For Missions' was included in the suggested Prayer Book as revised by the English Church Union (1923), and was incorporated in the 'Deposited Book' (1928). Professor Oscar Hardman inserts a prayer 'for all Missionaries Overseas', and a prayer 'for the Extension of the Church throughout the World' in his 'Prayer-Book for 1949'.

In the second place, the form of the old Litany was altered. While Hermann von Wied and Luther had left the scale of the Litany little changed, and Cranmer had elaborated it into a special service by the addition of the Lord's Prayer and other prayers, the Moravian version greatly expanded the body of the Litany proper. In the third place, the scope of the Litany was enlarged. This was due to the introduction of congregational singing, a characteristic Moravian innovation. It was because of its congregational character that the Litany appealed to the Brethren. This feature they now emphasised by introducing, for congregational use, verses from their own treasury of devotion, the Hymnbook.

The first English version of the Moravian liturgy was included in Part II of the English Hymnbook (1746). This was a literal rendering of the German version of 1744, but English versions of the Litany were to develop independently of those elsewhere. In 1749 the 'Church Litany of the Brethren' was printed as a document to support the 'Bill for the encouraging of people known by the name of *Unitas Fratrum* or "United Brethren" to settle in His Majesty's colonies', submitted to Parliament in that year. This version is substantially the Litany which appears in the great 1754 Hymnbook. It is included in the very rare *Acta Fratrum Unitatis in Anglia*. The Litany begins with the singing of 'Kyrie eleison', 'Christe eleison' by two choirs. The first choir sings the words 'Kyrie' and 'Christe', and the second choir 'eleison'. Both choirs then unite in the Lord's Prayer and Invocations. The deprecations are directed against such spiritual evils as sin, error, deceit, and hypocrisy. The obsecrations are more elaborate than in the Prayer Book. They include our Lord's 'childlike obedience', 'incessant troubles', 'temptations', 'watching and fasting', 'extremity in the garden', 'bonds and scourgings', 'thirst and drink of gall', and 'rest in the grave'. Provision is made during the obsecrations for Adult Baptism. Supplications for the Holy Catholic Church follow in much detail. Bishops and presbyters are prayed for. At various times during the supplications, provision is made for the ordination of pastors and the consecration of bishops. At the words, 'Bless the holy Matrimony', marriages are solemnised. At the words, 'Regenerate our children through water and the Holy Spirit', infants are baptised. At the words, 'Sprinkle all those who minister in the Sanctuary', deacons are ordained. At the words, 'Let Spirit and Fire rest upon their Testimony', messengers to the heathen are despatched. Here follows one of the most interesting parts of the Litany.

> *Keep our doors open among the Heathen, and open those that are still shut;*
> *Do not leave those Heathen desolate, from whom we are driven away;*
> *Have mercy on the Negroes, Savages, Slaves and Gipsies.*

The Litany ends with the *Agnus Dei* in English, Kyrie eleison, Christe eleison, and a great song of praise to God by both choirs.

It is interesting to note that at various parts of the Litany 'some proper antiphons are sung, or the music alone is heard'. Moravians have always maintained a high musical standard. Never have popular hymns been allowed to displace the chorales.

During the eighteenth and nineteenth centuries many hymn books were published, and the Litany was subject to constant amendment. In no two editions is the text identical. Editions appeared in 1769, 1789, 1801, 1809, 1826, 1836, 1838, 1844, 1849, 1854, 1869, 1886, 1911. Most of these books are in the

British Museum. *The Liturgy and Hymns authorised for use in the Moravian Church (Unitas Fratrum) in Great Britain and Ireland,* published in 1911, and a *Supplement to the Moravian Hymn Book,* published in 1940, were the two books in current use, until the publication of 'The Moravian Liturgy' in 1960.

The most radical revision of the Litany was that of 1911. It is of interest to compare the 'First Liturgy at Public Worship' (1911) with the previous edition of 1886. The two litanies are substantially the same, though there are many verbal alterations. Thus the invocation, 'Lord God, Son, thou Saviour of the World', becomes, 'O Son of God, thou Saviour of the World'. The 1911 Litany has a new deprecation very much in the spirit of a Church that continues to deplore sectarian bitterness, 'From hypocrisy and fanaticism . . . Save us, O Lord.' More ample provision is made in the 1911 liturgy for congregational singing. The Kyrie is removed in the 1911 edition from before to after the invocations. In mediaeval litanies it had been customary for the invocation of the Holy Trinity to be preceded by Kyrie eleison, etc. But this Kyrie was omitted by Cranmer. A characteristic Moravian supplication is included in the 1911 Litany, for time of war. 'Preserve the Unity of our Church; and let not the sight of a warring Christendom destroy any Missionary work among the non-Christian races.' Supplications are also inserted in this Litany for times of industrial strife and elections. The arrangement of concluding supplications is changed in the 1911 edition, so that the final petitions are for all those in need, and for God's mercy on His whole creation. In the 1911 version the versicle before the *Agnus* is 'O Christ, thou Son of God', instead of the version common to older Moravian litanies, 'O Christ, Almighty God'. The general effect of the 1911 revision is to improve the arrangement of the liturgy, simplify the presentation, modernise the language and enrich the subject matter.

The use of the Litany by the Moravians is the most striking characteristic of their worship. It is not surprising that of late years variations of the Litany have been forthcoming. The *Liturgy and Hymns* of 1911 includes a 'Second Liturgy at Public Worship'. This form is of interest because it is compiled from various sources, mostly non-Moravian, and includes collects and the General Thanksgiving from the Prayer Book. The

Supplement to the Moravian Hymn Book (1940) contains further additions of this kind. One responsive form is based on the petitions of the Lord's Prayer. Another form is compiled from various sources for use at Young People's services. Form of Prayer No. 5 is an adaptation of the 'Litany of the Life, Sufferings and Death of Jesus', composed almost certainly by Zinzendorf. The prayers are in the Litany form of responses; the petitions are for spiritual graces; and the Moravian characteristic of inserted hymn verses appears.

One of the remarkable features of the *Liturgy and Hymns* of 1911 is the influence of the Prayer Book. This is apparent in the 'Second Liturgy'. But the book also contains for occasional use 'An Alternative Form of Prayer', derived entirely from this source. This includes a General Confession (Morning Prayer); the prayer for all Conditions of Men (unaltered), and the prayer of Saint Chrysostom (unaltered; but without the title).

Moravian services are simple and dignified. It is singular to recall that at one epoch in the eighteenth century the Brethren became so enamoured of symbols, crosses, candles and vestments that George Whitefield concluded they were encouraging popery! It would seem that Moravians, in their tolerance, regard ritualism not with abhorrence but as belonging to the non-essentials of religion.

It is customary for the Lord's Supper to be celebrated once a month. During the last hymn, 'the Right Hand of Fellowship' is given. The preservation of this usage, so closely allied to the Kiss of Peace, is remarkable. The use of the hand is a peculiarity of the Syrian rites of the Church, derived from the Antiochene rite of St. James. A modern variation is the Hand-clasp in the rite of South India. But it has been observed by the Moravians since the old days at Herrnhut. How it arose among them is a matter of speculation. Bohemia was always subject to a certain influence from the East. Cyril and Methodius, the apostles of Christianity, came from the Byzantine Church. In the eighteenth century, Moravian missionaries were very active in the East, and Arvid Gradin consulted with the patriarchs of Constantinople and Jerusalem.

Not infrequently celebrations are preceded by a Love Feast, comprising hymns, prayers, and addresses. Love Feasts are held on other occasions, and have attracted Christians of diverse denominations. Revived in 1724 by the Moravians, and subsequently adopted by the Methodists, the Agape, rather than Holy Communion, may prove to be the ecumenical way of worship.

At one period in their history, Moravians observed the New Testament custom of footwashing. Before the administration of the Sacrament, the Elders washed the Brethren's feet, and the Eldresses washed the feet of the Sisters. This custom persisted until 1818.

The use of the Litany is extended even to occasional services. This is best seen in the Burial Service, and in Easter Morning Service. Holy Week is a season especially sacred to this Church. Moravians have been called the 'Easter People'. At Herrnhut, Zinzendorf inspired his co-religionists to assemble on Easter Morning to await the dawn. The lovely Easter Litany of 1749 was largely his composition. Today, the minister still gives the joyful cry, 'The Lord is risen'. To which the faithful reply, 'He is risen indeed'.

During the eighteenth and nineteenth centuries the Moravians cultivated an intense devotional life through the 'Settlement' system, which facilitated frequent services of worship on days other than Sunday. For these services special liturgic forms were provided. The first 'Liturgy Book', as it was called, was issued by Zinzendorf in 1744. It had many successors both in German and English. The first 'Liturgy Book' to appear in English was in 1770, and the latest in 1896. For the last forty years this book has been little used in the British Province of the Church. The decline in these special services is deplored in the preface to *Liturgic Hymns of the United Brethren*. Revised edition (1864). This Liturgy Book is planned to illustrate such themes as the Holy Trinity, and the Passion of our Lord. Alternate lines or verses are sung by liturgist, choir, and congregation. (The division of the congregation into 'choirs', an important feature of Zinzendorf's settlements, was a grouping according to sex, age, and condition, and had nothing to do with singing. Thus there were choirs of Single Brethren, Single Sisters, and Married people.) In the Litany of Praise to the Son in the 1864 book, the arrangement is seen by the following extract:

Liturgist: 'And who is that Word?'
All: 'Jesus Christ the Lord.'

Brethren: 'All the hosts of heav'n adore him,
      We with awe fall down before him,'
Sisters: 'And with ardour raise
      Songs of love and praise.'

Reference may perhaps be made to another Moravian liturgic custom very common until a century ago. This was the composition of Odes for special occasions. Not only were they written for the great Church Festivals and Moravian Memorial Days, but for church anniversaries, choir festivals, funerals, and even birthdays. Such odes provided verses for singing by congregation, choirs and soloists. A funeral ode of 1839 included chorales and responses.

In the British Province the 'Singing Meeting' has all but died out, though elsewhere still observed. This type of service was devoted entirely to the singing of hymns carefully selected to present the importance of a theme such as service, brotherly love, or mission work. Usually only the relevant verses were chosen.

In 1960 the Liturgy and Hymn Book Revision Committee, of which the Right Rev. E. W. Porter of the Moravian College, Manchester was secretary, issued *The Moravian Liturgy*. This book was prepared 'to meet the desire to have the services at present in full or partial use in the British Province assembled in a single volume'. It is an able compilation. The Preface disclaims any attempt to confine or restrict freedom in worship. But 'the Moravian Church values her liturgical tradition as a gift bestowed by her spiritual forefathers'.

Six orders of Public Worship are provided. Tradition is preserved in the 'Church Litany' (First Order). The other Orders have found favour with congregations during the present century. The Sixth Order contains the 'Christ Litany' of Zinzendorf. It is designed as an ante-Communion Service, and is placed immediately before the Lord's Supper, thus providing a complete Liturgy of the Word and the Upper Room. The First Order contains a Prayer for Christian Unity, in the noble Moravian manner. The Fourth includes the general confession (Morning Prayer) a general thanksgiving, the prayers for all Conditions of Men, and of Saint Chrysostom from the Prayer Book. Many collects and prayers in The Moravian Liturgy are derived from the same source. Prayer is addressed to Christ Himself in the Communion Service, which includes these words, 'And we most humbly beseech thee, O Lord, that with thy holy and life-giving spirit thou wilt bless and sanctify both us and these gifts of bread and wine.' Mention is made of the Love-feast, and a short office included entitled, 'The Cup of Covenant'. This originated in 1729 at Herrnhut when a young brother was called to the Mission Field. There are services for the Thanksgiving of Mothers, Infant and Adult Baptism, Confirmation, Marriage, and the Burial of the Dead. In the latter the Prayer Book commendation is included in a revised form; 'in sure and certain hope of the resurrection to eternal life of all believers'. In the Ordination Service the ancient form of presenting the candidate to the officiating bishop is restored. The three orders of bishops, presbyters, and deacons are retained.

Services for Christmas, Whitsuntide, and Trinity Sunday are introduced for the first time. Hymn verses, used as congregational responses, are employed to good effect. Thus in the Service for Good Friday, there are verses commemorating the trial before the Sanhedrin, the trial before Pilate, the mocking and the scourging, the sentence, the way to Calvary, Jesus on the Cross, the watchers by the Cross, and the burial. The Easter Service is of particular interest as it incorporates a Confession known as the 'Easter Morning Litany'. This Litany is associated with those early Easter Morning Services, held since 1733, and usually conducted in the burial ground. In the Service Book of 1759 it was very long. Later, it was to be shortened, and made appropriate for any season. The Nicene and Apostles' Creeds are included, following several Confessions of Faith in this liturgy.

In the development of Christian praise and prayer the Moravians have played a distinctive and distinguished role which deserves greater recognition. Above all, the claim made by Dr. Edward Langton and Dr. A. J. Lewis that the first international Protestant Church has a contribution to make to the Ecumenical Movement is not unjustified. The dream of the great Count–Bishop may yet come true.

CHAPTER VII

THE CONGREGATIONALISTS

IT is not to be expected that the heirs of the Pilgrim Fathers and Oliver's Ironsides would show a predilection for liturgical worship. Ever were the Independents powerful professors of spontaneous prayer. But it is at least significant of an awakened interest in liturgiology that Congregationalists have made some spasmodic but not unimportant experimentations. It is true that only some of the later books have been published with the authority of the Congregational Union of England and Wales. But the genius of Congregationalism is not denominationalism but the spiritual independence of the gathered church. In each communion of saints the Lord is in the midst. His promised presence in a gathered company covenanted together with duly appointed ministers constitutes a church. As a matter of propriety and order, a minister officiates at the Lord's Supper. But a layman could preside, though he would need authorisation from the Church Meeting. As Dr. Dale has said, an 'ordained minister is not necessary to give validity to the service'. This is no disparagement of the ministry. A local church, deprived of the services of a minister, need not be deprived of the Sacrament. For sacraments are acts of the Church.

The sixteenth century inaugurated a period of Reformation when the Bible was read with excitement. Men searched for the form of the Apostolic Church as guaranteed by the Holy Scriptures. And Congregationalism was reborn. It was not brought forth again without much labour and pain. Robert Browne was harried from town to town, and country to country, and only his kinship with Lord Burleigh saved his life. In 1593 Barrowe, Greenwood and Penry were put to death. The sailing of the *Mayflower* is now a romance. It was a grim ordeal then.

The 'troubles at Frankfort' brought before the Marian

refugees the problem of the final authority in the Church. Such questions were to lead to something worse than 'troubles' in the next century. As Fuller wrote during the Civil War: 'The penknives of that age are grown into swords in ours.' Dr. Albert Peel in his interesting *Story of Congregationalism* emphasises, and perhaps exaggerates, the influence of the hated Anabaptists. These religious revolutionaries were courageous enough to assert that the final authority in spiritual matters lay not with secular powers, but with those spiritual persons who, under Christ, make up the Church. One other factor of great importance contributed to the emergence of Congregationalism. During Mary's reign, secret meetings of Protestants had taken place in lonely warehouses and shops, in secluded woods, and in ships on the Thames. Dr. Dale has told of their significance. 'When Elizabeth came to the throne the blessedness of those secret meetings for worship would not soon be forgotten. Devout men and women had learnt that in a small company of Christian people, united to each other by strong mutual affection and a common loyalty to Christ, it was possible to realise in a wonderful way the joy and strength of the communion of saints; and that such an assembly, though it had only a weaver or wheelwright for its minister, might have a vivid consciousness of access to God through Christ, and might receive surprising discoveries of the divine righteousness and love.'

The gatherings of the devout for secret worship became more prevalent during Elizabeth's reign. Dr. Peel has shown that such congregations existed even before 1582 when Robert Browne wrote, 'The Kingdom of God was not to be begun by whole parishes, but rather of the worthiest, be they never so few.'

The predecessors of the Elizabethan Congregationalists were not infrequently called Brownists, after Robert Browne, or Barrowists, after Henry Barrowe. In three small books Browne made his notable contribution to the development of ecclesiastical organisation. Their titles are, *A Booke which sheweth the life and manners of all true Christians; A Treatise of Reformation without tarying for anie;* and *A Treatise upon the 23 of Mathewe.* These books set forth the Lordship of Christ and the independence of each church from any outside authority, the limitation of church membership to the 'elect', and the equality of all in the Christian fellowship. It is to be remembered that until the time of the Civil War congregations, though increasing, were not large. Generally they attracted only lowly folk.

It would seem that the majority of these congregations gave themselves to extemporaneous prayer. Henry Barrowe stigmatised the Prayer Book as 'well-nigh altogether idolatrous, superstitious, and popish'. But a small number of English dissidents are known to have used the Geneva Book about 1590. It is to be remembered that Browne himself lived for a time at Middelburg, and Congregational communities were at this period in exile in the Netherlands. It is not surprising, therefore, that some of the early Congregationalists accepted the Middelburg Prayer Book. Some sought a reformed liturgy solely in the words of Scripture. In his Introduction to *A Book of Public Worship, compiled for the use of Congregationalists* (1948), Dr. John Marsh insists that it is 'a cardinal error to think of the early Congregationalists as liturgical anarchists. They pleaded—and paid for liberty; but their worship was orderly. They were concerned, not that they might do as they pleased; but that they might worship as they ought. Standards of worship could not be fixed by the State; they had been determined by the Gospel. . . . They rejected the imposition by the State of a uniform liturgy, but accepted the constraint of the Gospel to a common liturgical structure.' That structure was derived from the Synagogue and the Upper Room. But it was extemporary prayer, called by Henry Barrowe 'a pouring forth of the heart unto the Lord', that was the secret of Independent piety. During the seventeenth century the Independents showed no liking for liturgies. Dr. John Owen condemned them as 'false worship used to defeat Christ's promise of gifts and God's spirit'. The attempt of the Stuart kings to enforce Prayer Book worship only increased their aversion. This has been explained by a distinguished Congregationalist. 'If a man declines to use a liturgy and you lop his ears and slit his nose to encourage him, human nature is so constituted that he is apt to grow more obstinate, and to conceive a quite unreasonable prejudice against the book.' The Prayer Book in the seventeenth century was becoming a symbol of tyranny. Moreover, the Act of Uniformity failed to provide an altenative liturgy, such as the Savoy Liturgy, which might have proved acceptable to the Independents. Henceforth they 'eliminated everything liturgical from their way of worship'.

The fortunes of the Independents had risen to impressive heights at the time of the Civil War. Numbered among them were men of illustrious fame. But the next century brought numerical and spiritual 'decay'. One great voice was raised. In his *Guide to Prayer* (1715), Isaac Watts, most gifted of Congregational ministers, urged the need of adequate preparation of prayer as 'a piece of holy skill'.

The decline was only temporary. The Evangelical revival brought expansion to Congregationalism in both England and America. Also it did much to break down the old Calvinism, though the Declaration of Faith issued in 1833 was Calvinistic, and Congregationalists abide still by 'the Crown Rights of the Redeemer'. But all creeds of Congregationalists are declaratory only. They are not imposed on any Congregationalist. For Independents the Congregationalists are still, though increasing co-ordination of the churches has come into being since the formation of the Congregational Union of England and Wales in 1831. Nor should it be forgotten that collaboration between churches has been part of the very being of an Independent Church. A deeper union than any ecclesiastical organisation binds Congregationalists together in this one fold. It is a common faith in the Living Christ.

LITURGIES OF THE CONGREGATIONALISTS

It would seem that the earliest attempt at a liturgy or directory to appear among the Congregationalists was published in 1847. It was entitled, *The Congregational Service Book: A form of Public Worship designed for the use of the Independent and Other Nonconformist Bodies in Great Britain*. A copy of this book is in the British Museum. *The Congregational Service Book* is a simple composition designed to introduce into public worship more Scripture, and more frequent psalms. Creeds are omitted as unnecessary, the only human composition permitted being the Te Deum. Free prayer is stipulated.

The Congregational Service Book is more of a directory than a liturgy. A much more elaborate compilation was published in

1856. This was, *A Biblical Liturgy for the use of Evangelical Churches and Homes*. It was edited by the Rev. David Thomas. Thomas was a man of some distinction, and the father of the better-known Urijah Thomas of Redland Park Congregational Church, Bristol. From 1844–77 he ministered at the Independent Church, Stockwell, London, and it was for the use of this church that the liturgy was devised, though other congregations adopted it. This prayer book ran into twelve editions. Thomas was one of the founders of University College, Aberystwith. He is to be remembered for the influence he exercised over two religious pioneers, Mrs. Catherine Booth, 'Mother of the Salvation Army', and Wilson Carlile, founder of the Church Army.

In his introduction Thomas complains of 'the low and unsatisfactory state of the devotional element in congregational services. The results are grievious. Hence, many Church people, who are attracted by our Pulpit, are repelled by our Altar.' There is not to be found in the *Biblical Liturgy* 'a human sentence or human word'. The twenty services are constructed from a central idea, such as God's Power and Wisdom, or Christ as King, Priest, and Prophet. Congregational responses are included in Scripture language. Free prayer is preserved. There are no occasional services.

Thomas's liturgy was based on the Bible. The next prayer book to be issued, *Liturgies for Divine Worship*, was indebted both to Bible and Prayer Book. The writer has not discovered a copy of the first edition of this book, which was translated into Telugu for the use of congregations in South India. The second edition includes prayers from Martineau's services in *Common Prayer for Christian Worship*. Thus it is later than 1862. It contains sixteen short services in the form of litanies and responsive readings. Considerable use is made of the collects and prayers of the Prayer Book. All services make provision for extemporary prayer. *Liturgies for Divine Worship* has neither author's name nor date. It may be presumed to be Congregationalist, as a copy was found in his vestry by the Rev. J. M. Todd at Great Yarmouth. It is not heavily doctrinal.

In 1867 a *Free Church Service Book* was edited by Christopher Newman Hall. Hall was minister of Surrey Chapel from 1854–92. Thence he removed to Christ Church, Westminster Bridge

Road. It is interesting to recall that one of the objects of his life was to promote closer relations between the Church of England and Dissent. Four million copies of his book, *Come to Jesus*, were published in forty languages.

Hall defended the use of liturgical worship for Congregationalists. 'Liturgical worship, or "common prayer", is surely more congregational than it is prelatical.' He believed that liturgical worship could promote Church union. 'These short services have been prepared in the hope that they may in some degree minister to the comfort, edification, and unity of the Church.' The five services are designed to supplement free prayer, with collects selected from the Prayer Book. *The Free Church Service Book* is the first of these liturgies to owe much to this source. Thus there is an Absolution Prayer by the minister, and a prayer for 'Ministers and Congregations' derived from the prayer for the 'Clergy and People'. The Nicene Creed is included. A shortened Communion office is taken from the Prayer Book.

A Form of Morning and Evening Service for the use of Free Churches was published in 1869 for the Congregational Church, Cheetham Hill, Manchester. It seems probable that the editor was G. W. Condor who was minister at that time, and the compiler of a hymn book adopted by the congregation. This book is of importance because it appears to be the first revision of the Prayer Book to be used by Congregationalists. In his preface the editor points out that he has made few alterations. He has avoided those needless repetitions which have troubled Evangelical Churchmen for so long. He assigns a place for free prayer between the Venite and Te Deum. This form comprises two services only. The Litany, which is considerably changed and abridged, is incorporated in the Evening Service. From the General Confession, 'miserable offenders' is omitted. The Absolution is removed, and the Benedicite left out. The unscriptural clause, 'He descended into Hell' is expunged from the Apostles' Creed. The sentence, 'strengthen her that she may vanquish and overcome all her enemies' is deleted from the prayer for the Queen. The 'good estate of the Catholick Church' becomes the 'good estate of thy Church universal' in the prayer for all Conditions of Men. The title 'Saint Chrysostom' is omitted before the prayer.

Two revisions of the Prayer Book soon followed. It is possible that *Forms submitted for the use of Nonconformist Churches* (1870) was edited by a Congregationalist. It is an abridgement of Anglican services, retaining extemporaneous prayer. There are no occasional services. A revision entitled *The Liturgy of the Church of England* (abridged), was published in 1874 by David Thomas.

In 1880 was published one of the most celebrated prayer books by a Dissenting divine. Fifty years have passed since Dr. John Hunter's *Devotional Services for Public Worship* reached a final form, but it still commands a small but steady sale. The occasional offices are in frequent use among Free Church and Church of Scotland ministers. Other prayer books have drawn freely from it. It was compiled for use at Trinity Church, Glasgow, where the editor had two famous ministries. It was introduced to London during Hunter's short ministry at the King's Weigh House. At this church, Congregationalists were treated to the novel sight of a mixed choir in surplices. The final form of *Devotional Services* includes ten orders of service for morning and evening, two abbreviated services, and a Week Evening Service. There are also orders for the Lord's Supper, Baptism, Dedication (for the admission of the baptised to full communion), Marriage, the Visitation of the Sick, the Burial of the Dead, and a service of Commemoration for the Faithful Departed. Included are general prayers, and prayers for the Christian Year. The ten full Sunday services follow a pattern of Scripture Sentences inviting to worship, prayer of invocation, general confession, hymn, Old Testament lesson, psalms, New Testament lesson, the Beatitudes or Commandments, extemporary prayer, anthem or canticle or hymn, prayer of intercession with the Lord's Prayer, hymn, collect, sermon, offertory, prayer, hymn and benediction. The influence of the Prayer Book is conspicuous. From the Anglican General Confession are omitted the words, 'And there is no health in us', 'miserable offenders', and 'for his sake'. 'Catholick Church' becomes the 'Church Universal' in the prayer for all conditions of men. Worshippers are asked to kneel for prayer. Extemporary prayer is stipulated, since 'the ideal of public worship is the union in one service of free and liturgical prayer.' The Lord's Supper embodies some features of the Anglican office. Later, Dr. Orchard was unwilling to celebrate Communion in this form at the King's Weigh House, though not averse to the rest of his predecessor's book. He disliked the departure from historic form. There are no manual acts. The words of delivery are, 'Let us eat of this bread in remembrance of Christ; and may the life which was in Him be in us also', and 'Let us drink of this cup in remembrance of Christ; and may the spirit in which He died be our spirit'. No sponsors are required for baptism, save the parents. It is of interest to note that Hunter provides as alternative to the Triune formula in baptism, 'In the faith and fellowship of the Church of Christ, I dedicate thee to God, our Father in heaven.'

In the last decade of the nineteenth century two further books were published. They were *Devotional Services for use in Mill Hill Chapel* (1895), and a book entitled *Let us Pray*. The latter was at one period in frequent use among ministers as a directory. It was a handbook of selected collects and forms of prayer by two well-known Congregational ministers, C. Silvester Horne and T. Herbert Darlow. *Let us Pray* contains outline orders of service for morning and evening, and services for Infant Baptism, and Holy Communion. Most of the collects and prayers are from the Prayer Book.

An interesting liturgical form came into use at Cheetham Hill Church, Manchester. Dr. P. T. Forsyth published *Intercessory Services for Aid in Public Worship* in 1896 when minister of Emmanuel Congregational Church, Cambridge. But, although unprinted, these services were in use during a previous ministry at Cheetham Hill. Dr. Forsyth granted the need for free prayer in the free churches, but urged the value of forms for intercessory prayer. 'The intercessory part of public prayer is not in its nature an outpouring of the spirit-stirred soul in the name, and in the midst, of a like-minded and like-moved church.' The book consists of seven very fine litanies, with sung responses by the congregation. P. T. Forsyth was described by Lord Morley as 'one of the most brilliant minds in Europe'. He appears to have anticipated much of the work of Karl Barth.

Prayer and Praise (1914) compiled for the Penge Congregational Church by the Rev. E. D. Cecil is still in use at that church. It contains morning and evening services for each Sunday of the month. Much of the material is drawn from the

Prayer Book, particularly from Mattins and Evensong. Provision is made for extemporary prayer in all services. There are orders for the chief Festivals, the Sacraments, Marriage and Burial.

Perhaps the best representative of a group of similar books adopted by Congregational Churches is *Orders of Worship* compiled by H. E. Brierley for Immanuel Church, Southbourne, Bournemouth. A third and revised edition was issued in 1950 by the Rev. N. A. Turner-Smith. This book is indebted to Dr. Forsyth's *Intercessory Services* and to the Prayer Book. Morning and evening services are provided for five Sundays in the month. The services include the General Thanksgiving and General Confession (unaltered) from the Prayer Book. Litanies are incorporated with congregational responses.

In 1923 George H. Russell of Matlock published *Intercession Services for Congregational Use in Public Worship*. This form was commended in a Foreword by Dr. J. H. Jowett, C.H. 'The prayers have greatly enriched the worship of one Church, indeed, they have given its worship a uniqueness among the Churches. . . . They certainly meet a very real need in the worship of the non-episcopal Churches.' The book comprises twenty-two short services, in the form of prayers and litanies, built upon a single theme. Thus there are services 'For the Coming of God's Kingdom', 'For International Peace', and 'For Social and Industrial Peace'. The editor acknowledges indebtedness to Principal P. T. Forsyth. Thus his sixteenth service includes parts of Dr. Forsyth's sixth service. Mr. Russell also draws from the prayer books of Dr. John Hunter and Dr. W. E. Orchard. An interesting feature of his book is the Litany in the thirteenth service written by the Rev. Simeon Singer of the Liberal Jewish Synagogue, London. It will be noted that these services are additions to, and not substitutions for, free prayer.

The Rodborough Bede Book is not so much a liturgy as a rich mine of prayers and litanies. The Rev. C. E. Watson sought to combine free prayer with a liturgical element, so varied in character as to avoid the tedium of repetition. In 1878 the Unitarian Robert Crompton Jones had attempted something on these lines with his thirty short services. But the *Bede Book* is more ambitious. Collects, prayers and litanies are grouped together for the opening of services ('Fore Bedes'); for the middle of services ('Mid Bedes'); and for the closing of services ('End Bedes'). A vast amount of material has been made serviceable by the simple method of numbering the offices consecutively as with a book of hymns. It is interesting to observe that the editor has utilised the Prayer Book, the services of Dr. Hunter and Dr. Orchard and the prayers of Martineau.

Services for Derby Street Congregational Church, Bolton, were published by R. Lawrence Jones in 1943. The ten orders for Sunday include many responses for minister and congregation. Some collects and prayers are taken from the Prayer Book. The editor quotes with approval the words of Heiler in *The Spirit of Worship.* 'There is arising, even in Protestant circles which for centuries have been opposed to liturgies, a strong feeling of the need for liturgical forms. The liturgical movement today is a general Christian movement which cuts across all Confessional divisions. Christianity is weary of individualism, which weakens and divides; it is striving to escape the narrow bondage of the subjective into the freedom of the objective, the universal; from the limitations of the isolated individual to the fullness and strength of the great Community.'

Responsals (1947), by E. R. Micklem and Irene M. Shewell Cooper, Ministers of the Congregational Church, Gerrards Cross, is a series of acts of prayer and worship designed to give congregations active participation in worship, without the formality of a liturgy or the exclusion of free prayer. Skilful use is made of the Bible in this charming book. Thus in the responsals for Christmas, Good Friday, Easter, Ascension Day and Whit Sunday, the gospel narratives are presented with appropriate responses by the people.

The various prayer books of individual Congregational churches have been examined in detail so as to give the reader some conception of the extent and character of the liturgical movement in Congregationalism. This is necessary because there is no 'Congregational Church' analogous to the 'Presbyterian Church' or the 'Methodist Church'. There are Congregational churches. And each individual congregation has the right to adopt the mode of worship it prefers. It would seem that it is not uncommon for Congregational services to contain a liturgical element, such as the litanies used by the late Arthur Pringle at Purley.

Congregational churches are federated in the Congregational Union of England and Wales, and the *Book of Congregational Worship* published in 1920 is of importance as the first prayer book issued by the Union. The use of this book is optional. It is semi-liturgical in character, preserving the practice of extemporary prayer in each of the ten orders for Sunday worship. The editors, among whom was Dr. P. T. Forsyth, made considerable use of the Prayer Book, the prayers of Martineau, and the services of Dr. John Hunter and Dr. W. E. Orchard. These very simple services include litanies, responses, and prayers ancient and modern. The Order of Holy Communion, which is designed to follow the ordinary Sunday service, begins with a hymn followed by the comfortable words, an invitation taken from the Prayer Book, a confession of sins compiled from the Psalms, and the *sursum corda* and preface from the Prayer Book. There follow words of institution, a consecration prayer, with commemoration of the Redemption, thanksgiving for the benefits of the Passion, and a self-oblation from the First Prayer Book of King Edward VI. The service ends with silent prayer, distribution, and Communion. The *Book of Congregational Worship* contains services of Baptism, Marriage, Burial and Ordination, with laying on of hands. An excellent feature of the book is the number of occasional prayers and collects, with a Lectionary that includes some lessons from the Apocrypha. It is noticeable that from the Anglican General Confession are omitted the words, 'And there is no health in us', and 'miserable offenders'. 'Catholic Church' is retained in the prayer for all Conditions of Men.

A Manual for Ministers was produced by the Congregational Union in 1936. Dr. Sidney M. Berry in his Foreword welcomed the tendency of the Churches to make use of liturgical material as supplementing free prayer. Acknowledgements are given to the service books of Dr. John Hunter and Dr. W. E. Orchard. Use is freely made of the Prayer Book. The *Manual* provides sentences, collects and prayers to be used at the minister's discretion. There are two orders of Holy Communion, and services of Baptism, Marriage, Burial and the Visitation of the Sick. These offices do not present any features of especial interest. Orders are included for Christmas Day, Good Friday, Easter Day and Whitsuntide, and for the Ordination and Induction of ministers. The *Manual* emphasises the importance of the diaconate in Congregationalism by an Order for the Dedication of Deacons. The deacons are not ordained. They are given the right hand of fellowship by the minister. A similar type of service is included for the Dedication of Sunday School Teachers. It is significant of an increasing awareness of the importance of social service that the book includes, 'An Act of Dedication' for those engaging in that work. There is even an Order for the Opening of a Church Bazaar! Special services are included for Foreign Missions, Hospital Sunday and Peace Sunday. A Lectionary is appended.

The *Book of Congregational Worship* (1920) adhered to prevailing custom. In 1948 the Congregationalists showed their awareness of liturgical thought in the Reformed Churches by the production of *A Book of Public Worship, compiled for the use of Congregationalists*. Here it is stated explicitly that 'Congregationalist worship is to be understood in terms of Holy Communion, not of Mattins or Evensong'. The editors were John Huxtable, John Marsh, Romilly Micklem, and James Todd. This work remains true to the Congregationalist tradition. 'It is to be understood as a "Directory of Public Worship", and not a "Book of Common Prayer".' The sources of *A Book of Public Worship* are illuminating. They include the historic Middelburg Prayer Book and Baxter's Savoy Liturgy. Other sources fall into two groups, Congregational and Presbyterian. The first consists of the service books of Dr. John Hunter and Dr. W. E. Orchard, together with the *Book of Congregational Worship*, 1920. The second consists of *Euchologion*, the *Book of Common Order* of 1928, the *Book of Common Order* of 1940, and the *Presbyterian Church of England Directory of Public Worship*. There has been close contact between English Congregationalism and the Presbyterian Church of England of recent years. Many Congregational liturgists are in agreement with those Presbyterians who aver that the Eucharist is the heart of worship.

A Book of Public Worship supplies five orders for Sunday. These vary in detail. But all contain hymns and Scripture sentences, with prayers of confession. Lessons from the Old and New Testaments are interspersed with psalms or canticles. Prayers of thanksgiving and intercession end with the Lord's Prayer. Offerings are followed by prayers of dedication.

Prayers for illumination precede the sermon. The sermon is succeeded by prayer and praise, or praise and prayer, with the blessing. Congregationalists share with other Reformed churchmen the belief that preaching itself is a sacrament. 'True preaching "contemporises" the Gospels and that is sacramental action' (Preface). Four services of Holy Communion are provided, each including an epiclesis. Directions are given in the rubrics for the fraction and also for the elevation of the cup.

The most important features of the occasional services are as follows. As Congregationalists believe that the right of administering sacraments belongs to the whole Church, it is required that baptisms should take place in Church during Public Worship. The proper sponsors are held to be the parents who speak for themselves only. In the Ordination Service the Presiding Minister uses familiar words, 'In the name of the Lord Jesus Christ, the King and Head of the Church, we are met together', etc. The laying on of hands is appointed to take place during the Ordination Prayer. But Congregational practice diverges here from historic Presbyterian. The Ordaining clergyman is assisted by lay representatives of the Church. Women are not excluded from the diaconate, nor from the ministry.

In fulfilment of a hope expressed in the introduction to *A Book of Public Worship* a companion volume was issued in 1951. This was entitled *Prayers and Services for Christian Festivals*. It is significant of a changing outlook in modern Dissent that a study of Congregational worship should include a book for encouraging a fuller observance of the Christian Year. It would seem that gradually the Free Churches are recovering a lost inheritance now that the ancient dread of Rome is a thing of the past. Modern Free Churchmen, though faithful to their Protestant witness, are more conscious of belonging to the Holy Catholic Church than were their fathers.

Prayers and Services for Christian Festivals is edited by the Rev. James M. Todd, formerly of Emmanuel Congregational Church, West Wickham, Kent, one of the editors of *A Book of Public Worship*. Mr. Todd is in the true line of Congregational liturgists for his purpose is not to recommend formal or fixed liturgies, but to provide suitable examples of forms of services and prayers.

This book is divided into three parts. Part I contains selections of Scripture sentences and prayers for the ordinary services of the Church. Such services include Scripture sentences, invocations, adorations, confessions, supplications, thanksgivings and intercessions. They are arranged for Advent, Christmas, Epiphany, Lent, Palm Sunday, Good Friday, Easter Day, Ascension, Whit Sunday, Trinity, All Saints' and for such occasions as a Church Anniversary, Dedication Sunday, Missionary Sunday, Bible Sunday, Old Year, New Year, Harvest Thanksgiving, and Remembrance Day.

Part II contains three short orders of Holy Communion for Christmas Day, Easter Day, and Whit Sunday. In many Congregational Churches it is customary to hold early morning celebrations on these days, and the orders are designed with that in mind. The order is as follows:

Call to worship
Hymn
Prayer
Confession (silent)
Old Testament, Epistle, and Gospel
Sermon
Prayers of Intercession
Te Deum or Hymn
Offerings
Record of the Institution
Setting aside of the elements
Lift up your hearts, etc.
It is meet, right, etc., and
ending 'Therefore with angels, etc.
'Holy, Holy, Holy', etc.
Prayer with epiclesis
The Lord's Prayer
The Fraction and Elevation
The Distribution
Prayer
Blessing.

Part III contains services of an experimental nature, designed to supplement the regular services of the Church. They include the Festival of Nine Lessons and Carols, services for Christmas Eve, Epiphany, any day of Holy Week, each day of Holy Week,

Easter Praise, Ascension Day, Whitsuntide, and a Watch-night Service.

In 1959 a committee appointed by the Congregational Union of England and Wales produced *A Book of Services and Prayers*. It justifies its claim to be a 'comprehensive guide to the conduct of Divine Worship, mainly in churches of the Congregational Order'. It is no formal liturgy. Rather is it a help to ministers who are provided with outlines of services, and an extensive anthology of prayers for all occasions, including the Christian Year. Its most interesting feature is the Lectionary of the Church of South India.

CHAPTER VIII

THE BAPTISTS

No study of the great Free Churches would be complete without some reference to the Baptists. It must be admitted, however, that these uncompromising Protestants have never displayed any real liking for prayer-book worship. It is true that of recent years there have been some moves in a liturgical direction. But, in general, Baptists feel that such changes are not in accord with their tradition or history.

The Baptists are staunch Free Churchmen, and their devotion to the Holy Scriptures is unassailable. It has been seen how the translation of the Bible into the vernacular gave rise to many questions concerning the polity of the Church during the sixteenth and seventeenth centuries. Hence arose those groups of Independents or Separatists who refused to accept the Elizabethan Church settlement and who suffered accordingly varying degrees of persecution. Some sought a purer form of church government and worship in the more tolerant atmosphere of Holland.

The beginnings of the Baptist denomination, as distinct from the Independent, are to be found in connection with the Amsterdam Church. There had come over with the Gainsborough exiles a former Fellow of Christ's College, Cambridge, John Smyth, who had been lecturer or preacher to the city of Lincoln. This appointment he had lost because of his Separatist views. It was in Amsterdam that Smyth developed his position. In 1609 he published *The Character of the Beast* in which he set forth Baptist teaching. Smyth held that infants ought not to be baptised. He saw no authority for such a practice in the New Testament, nor any examples of it. He contended that it was the command of Christ that people should first be taught, and only then baptised. Strongly maintaining the Arminian position, Smyth parted company with the Independents, who were

Calvinistic. 'God', he declared, 'doth not predestinate any man to destruction.' Further he maintained that 'infants are conceived and born in innocency without sin, and so dying are undoubtedly saved'.

Smyth had the courage of his convictions. Having baptised himself, he baptised his followers including the famous Thomas Helwys. Together they formed the first English Baptist Church. The 'declaration of faith' of this church published two years later denied the right of the State to meddle with the consciences of men. This is the first known declaration of absolute liberty of conscience in any confession of faith.

Smyth died in Holland in 1612. Helwys returned to England and in Newgate Street, London, established the first Baptist church on English soil. This little church was the first in England to proclaim absolute liberty of religion and conscience. This notable and noble event in Christian history was the direct outcome of the Baptist belief that conversion is an experience between a man and his Maker and, as such, beyond the competency of any external authority. 'Christ only is the King and lawgiver of the Church and Conscience' (Smyth's confession of 1612).

It is unnecessary for the purposes of this brief study to follow the fortunes of the Baptists who now claim to be the largest Protestant communion in the world. The church in Newgate Street was the origin of the 'General Baptist' denomination. 'General Baptists' were so called because they repudiated Calvin's doctrine of the predestination of the elect only. They held that Christ died for all men in general. A quite distinct denomination, known as the Calvinistic or 'Particular' Baptist Church, had its beginnings in 1633 at the Independent Jacob church in Southwark. Particular Baptists believed that Christ died for the elect and for no other.

Neither General Baptists nor Particular Baptists were at first pledged to immersion at Baptism, and indeed rarely practised it. W. T. Whitley says that John Smyth, the 'Se-Baptist', applied water to his own forehead. It was not until 1644 that the Particular Baptists in a Confession of Faith declared, 'The way and manner of dispensing this ordinance the Scripture holds out to be dipping or plunging the whole body under water.' General Baptists followed suit some years later.

The conflict between Calvinists and Arminians, Free Communionists and Strict Communionists, agitated the Baptists for many years to come. But ever their root principle of baptism only on conversion has given to their mission cohesion, a positive character, and a unifying strength.

So devoted are Baptists to certain doctrines that they have a clear concept of the character of the Christian Church and the nature of the Church's mission to the world. Admission to the Christian Church, as stated by them, is permissible only on fixed terms. These are repentance, faith in the ever-blessed Trinity, confession of Christ, and believers' baptism. The Church is God's agent in the world during this age. The mission of the Church is to win the world for God. The members of the Church must be thoroughly in earnest about this duty. The Church is not an hereditary corporation into which every child is born. It is the society of disciples prepared to subordinate everything to the purposes of God. The Christian must be a personal evangelist.

It is significant that Smyth's first publication after his disavowal of holy orders concerned the visible Church. In reply to inquiries from Suffolk, he declared: 'The churches of the apostolique constitution consisted of saints only. . . . The true ministerie of the apostolique institution was by election, approbation, and ordination of that particular holy people whereto they did administer.' Then follows an important passage bearing directly on this study. 'The true worship of the apostolique institution proceeded meerly from the Spirit, having no outward help of devised forms of prayers, exhortations, psalms, and ceremonies.'

The Baptist disinclination for any formal liturgy has been expressed on occasion with robust vigour. Thus Vavasor Powell, who suffered much for the 'Good Old Cause' after the Restoration, and who died in prison under Charles II, strongly attacked the Book of Common Prayer. His antipathy was directed not to any detail in particular but to the whole principle of an authorised prayer book.

The objection of Baptists to fixed and formal modes of worship was in evidence again towards the end of the seventeenth century. Rather surprisingly the London churches pioneered the singing of hymns at worship. They led the way from versified psalms to new compositions, partly experimental, chiefly doctrinal. This innovation excited all Baptist circles. In 1689 the General Baptists decided that the use of a hymn book was a rejection of the leading of the Spirit. This was quite in the vein of John Smyth. But the Particular Baptist Assembly decided that no principle was involved. In 1691 Benjamin Keach printed three hundred hymns for general use. Other hymns for baptismal and communion services were forthcoming.

Understandably the influence of John Smyth has endured among his co-religionists for, as Mandell Creighton said of him, 'none of the English Separatists had a finer mind or a more beautiful soul.' Smyth objected to the use of any book in public worship. This applied not only to a liturgy, but to psalms sung from a book, and sermons read by a preacher. As for the Bible Smyth thought it should be read publicly on Sunday, but only as a preparation for worship. Worship, he considered, technically began only after all books had been laid aside. 'We hold', said Smyth in his treatise on 'The differences of the Churches of the separation' (1608), 'that the worship of the new testament properly so called is spiritual proceeding originally from the heart: and that reading out of a book (though a lawful ecclesiastical action) is no part of spiritual worship, but rather the invention of the man of sin it being substituted for a part of spiritual worship.'

Objection to the use of prayer books has been general among Baptists since the time of Smyth. But of late years there has been a tendency, in some quarters, to favour a liturgical element in worship. The able and masterful Secretary of the Baptist Union, the late Dr. J. H. Shakespeare, finally succeeded in incorporating into *The Baptist Church Hymnal* (the revised edition of 1900) a series of intercessions in poetical form. These metrical litanies were the work of a Presbyterian minister, the Rev. Thomas Benson Pollock (1836–96). The writer has been assured by the Principal of Regent's Park College, Oxford, that these litanies are not in use in any Baptist church. Nor can Principal Child understand why they should have been included in the book. It is somewhat curious that part of Mr. Pollock's Litany, published in 1870, has found its way into the *Church Hymnal*, the official hymn book of the Church of Ireland. It is little, if ever, used. This Litany must have attained considerable popularity at one period, for some verses (slightly amended) are still included in the Unitarian hymnal *Hymns of Worship* as a children's hymn. It is evident, however, that neither Baptists nor Anglicans have favoured this singular Presbyterian importation. Dr. Shakespeare was a man given to innovations. J. C. Carlile described him as 'an ecclesiastic quite unlike any leader Baptists had known'. Many Nonconformists considered him altogether too fond of the order and traditionalism of the Church of England. Mr. Pollock's metrical litanies are arranged in the *Baptist Church Hymnal* (1900) under such headings as the Holy Spirit, the Love of God, Penitence, and the Beatitudes. The latter includes sung responses by the congregation. A typical verse of these litanies reads,

> *Jesu, from Thy throne on high,*
> *Far above the bright blue sky,*
> *Look on us with loving eye.*
> *Hear us, Holy Jesu.*

Mr. Pollock's litanies were not included in the 1933 revision of the *Baptist Church Hymnal*.

Although the Baptists have shown a marked reluctance to accept liturgical innovation isolated churches have developed a liturgical tradition of their own. Among these is the Hamstead Road Baptist Church, Handsworth, Birmingham. *Services for Public Worship* were prepared by the minister of this beautiful church, the Rev. Henry Bonner. This liturgy, which was published about 1890, is of importance as being the first published book of services ever used by a Baptist church. A revised edition was issued in 1900. Acknowledgements are made to R. Crompton Jones, as also to Sadler and Martineau. Some of the collects from Canon Bright's *Ancient Collects* are included. The liturgy is enriched by many fine prayers, and gives evidence of the propriety and cultivated taste of the compiler. But there is little doctrinal emphasis, and nothing that would appear to be significantly Baptist. There are ten Sunday services for the five Sundays of the month. The general pattern, which is varied slightly, is opening Scriptural sentences, some sung responses (mutual salutation and *sursum corda*), prayers, the Lord's Prayer (sung), versicles, psalm, lesson, hymn, lesson, Commandments or Beatitudes (with responses), chant, prayers or Litany, anthem or hymn, prayers, hymn, sermon, optional extemporary prayer, offertory, responses, hymn, and blessing. Very little material is taken from the Book of Common Prayer apart from the Litany which is appended to these services in a revised form. The congregation is directed to kneel for prayer. The service of Holy Communion is prefaced with the words: 'This is verily and indeed partaking of Christ, if a man have His Spirit.' The service is Nonconformist in character, the minister saying, 'Almighty God, our heavenly Father . . . grant that we, receiving this bread and this wine as symbols of His broken body and shed blood.' The liturgy includes four short services for children, one being for Christmas. The occasional prayers and collects include some for missions.

A revised and larger version of Dr. Bonner's book was edited by his successor, the Rev. Frederick C. Spurr, in 1930. This book, entitled *Come, Let Us Worship*, is still in use at morning service at Hamstead Road Church. An important feature of this book is the evidence it affords of an increasing awareness of the significance of the Christian Year in Free Churches. There are special services, with many congregational responses, for Christmas Day, Easter Day, and Whit Sunday. There are also collects and Scripture sentences for Advent, Palm Sunday, Good Friday, and the Ascension. Mr. Spurr's revision is proof of a more perfect comprehension of the Holy Communion as the most important of Christian services. It is stated, specifically, that this service 'is not intended as an addendum to the ordinary Morning or Evening Service, but as a Service complete in itself'. Marriage and Burial services are included in this liturgy. The Christening service is an obvious omission from a Baptist prayer book. The Burial service assumes that the dead child is saved. 'It is well with the child.'

It was the hope of the Rev. F. W. Spurr that wide use would be made of his book in the denomination. But in this he was disappointed.

A more successful attempt to provide the Baptists with a book of prayers was made by the Rev. D. Tait Patterson. Mr. Patterson was induced to publish the services he had introduced into his church at Dewsbury. They appeared under the title of *The Call to Worship*. This liturgy has run into five editions, four British, and one American. (First edition, 1930.)

Mr. Patterson does not provide a detailed service. He contents himself with offering a wide variety of material from which ministers may construct their own services. In the second edition of *The Call to Worship* the thirty-seven responsive litanies are omitted. Later in the same year they were republished separately. In its present form *The Call to Worship* has had a marked success in Great Britain and the Commonwealth. But the responsive litanies have never found much favour.

The Call to Worship is no formal liturgy. In the words of the Preface, 'It is a contribution to a conception of public worship in which the worshipper takes a definite part.' The musical portions of the book are selected and arranged by Sir George Dyson, Mus. Doc. The compiler draws on many sources for his material. These include Hunter's *Devotional Services* and Orchard's *Divine Services*. Both Bible and Prayer Book are used extensively. Part I of *The Call to Worship* consists of a large number of Scripture sentences for introduction to worship, with suitable responses by the congregation. These sentences are arranged into such convenient themes as 'Praise and Thanksgiving', and 'Repentance'. Special attention is paid to the Christian Year. Thus there are sentences for Advent, Christmas, Lent, Good Friday, Easter, Ascension, and Whit Sunday. The second part is devoted to 'Great Catholic Prayers of the Church'. This section is derived largely from the Prayer Book, and includes 'A general Thanksgiving', the prayer 'for all Conditions of Men', and the general confession from Morning Prayer. In this prayer the words 'and there is no health in us', and 'miserable offenders' are optional. The general confession from the Communion office is included, with the words 'provoking most justly Thy wrath and indignation against us' in brackets for omission if desired. The Te Deum, Magnificat, Benedictus, and Nunc Dimittis are also included, along with the *Sursum Corda* and *Gloria in Excelsis* from the Communion office. Many prayers and collects from the Prayer Book are included, arranged in groups, some being for the Christian Year. The third part consists of sentences and prayers for the Dedication of Children, the Baptism of Believers, the Lord's Supper, Marriage, Burial, and Ordination. There is no laying on of hands in the Ordination Service, which concludes with the Lord's Supper. These services owe something to the Prayer

Book but are in no sense revisions. The fourth and fifth parts comprise many litanies with responses by the congregation. These include litanies for Christmas Day and Good Friday. There is also a Missionary Litany.

The first service book to come into general use among Baptists was *A Manual for Free Church Ministers*, edited by Dr. G. P. Gould, and Dr. J. H. Shakespeare. It was mainly Dr. Shakespeare's work. The *Manual* contains services for the Solemnisation of Matrimony, the Burial of the Dead, the Dedication of Infants, the Baptism of Believers, and the Lord's Supper. There is also a small selection of hymns suitable for each service. These simple but dignified services are constructed on a pattern familiar to the Free Churches, and owe very little to the Prayer Book. In the order for the Burial of the Dead the words of the commendation are changed from, 'to take unto himself the soul of our dear brother here departed', to 'call hence the soul of our departed brother'. In the order for the Dedication of Infants the minister, having demanded the name of the child, says, 'N. the Lord bless thee and keep thee. . . .' The order for the Baptism of Believers contains a short address in which reference is made 'to the strange deviation from primitive practice which is manifested by those who in this matter think not with us'. Baptism is then explained as a profession of discipleship, the declaration of salvation received, and an act of obedience. At the immersion the minister says, 'On thine own desire, and on a profession of repentance towards God and faith in our Lord Jesus Christ, I baptise thee, "N", into the name of the Father, and of the Son, and of the Holy Ghost.'

Dr. Shakespeare's *Manual* has been succeeded in more recent times by *A Minister's Manual* compiled by Dr. M. E. Aubrey. This manual is similar to the previous book in essential details. The inclusion of some sentences, for optional use, from the Book of Wisdom in the Burial Service would seem to show a changing attitude of Free Churchmen to the Apocrypha.

It is usual for the Lord's Supper to be observed in English Baptist churches, after the first evening service of the month. Sunday morning celebrations are also common. A Baptist celebration commemorates the simple meal in the Upper Room, and constitutes the supreme expression of the fellowship of the

Church as created by, and maintained in, the fellowship of individual believers with Christ. In both *A Manual for Free Church Ministers* and *A Minister's Manual* the words of institution are followed by a prayer of thanksgiving prior to the distribution. It should be noted, however, that in his book, *The Life and Faith of the Baptists*, Principal H. Wheeler Robinson outlines a Baptist Communion service as consisting of hymn, prayer of confession, invocation of the Holy Spirit, words of institution and prayer of thanksgiving, distribution of the elements, prayer for the communion of saints, followed by the collection for the poor of the Church, and a closing hymn. In addition to their own manuals, Baptist ministers frequently use the Congregational book, *A Manual for Ministers* (Independent Press).

In 1937 the Rev. J. Isaiah Jones of Christ Church, Aston, published *Readings for Worship*. This book is designed for use in Young People's services, as also for that part of the ordinary Sunday morning service sometimes devoted to children in the Free Churches. Specially selected passages from the Scriptures are read by a leader and the children. These passages have been chosen with discrimination. But what makes this book remarkable is that some selections are taken from the Apocrypha, and some from the poets and religious writers. This book is in use at Aston, but does not appear to have been adopted by other congregations.

Although liturgical experimentation is not unknown among the Baptists it would seem that prayer-book worship is not likely to become popular. The one considerable change in Baptist worship of recent years is the adoption, in many churches, of the 'responsive prayer' in place of the 'long prayer'. Occasionally some congregation adopts a semi-liturgical service, as at Victoria Road Church, Leicester. Morning service, at this church, includes some versicles and canticles together with litanies taken from many sources. It is interesting to recall that when the Victoria Road Church was built in 1866 there were rumours that the Book of Common Prayer would be adopted. This would have made history in John Smyth's denomination.

CHAPTER IX

CHURCHES OF CHRIST

IT may be that in the annals of Christian history the twentieth century will be remembered as the period in which mankind, in agonised labour, brought forth the genesis of World Peace and a United Christendom. For if an American statesman could publish a treatise on 'One World', Protestant divines could convoke a World Council of Churches, and a Roman pontiff a second Vatican Council. Christian men, of all sorts and conditions, are giving new thought to the Apostolic injunction, 'One Lord, one faith, one baptism', and are aware of the divisions of Christendom with a growing unease.

The importance of the group of churches known in this country as 'Churches of Christ', and in America as 'The Disciples', is their unceasing advocacy of a united Christendom. For a century and a half they have been the pioneers of the Ecumenical movement. Not content with a lament for the rending of the seamless robe these New Testament Christians have taken to heart the words of St. Paul in 1 Cor. i and iii, and have insisted that sectarianism is sin.

Their origins are to be found among the Glasites and Scotch Baptists of the eighteenth century. But it was in the nineteenth century that the Churches of Christ attained maturity. Two men, father and son, were the dominating influences. Thomas Campbell was born in County Down, and was educated for the Presbyterian ministry at Glasgow University. In 1807 he emigrated to Pennsylvania. There he formulated basic principles: 'Where the Scriptures speak we speak, and where they are silent we are silent', and 'Christian liberality and Christian union on the basis of the Bible'. His celebrated *Declaration and Address*, which renounced all systems of theology as tests of fellowship, was published in 1809. This year has been taken to be the decisive date in the evolution of the Movement.

Having withdrawn from the Presbyterian Church because of bitter opposition, Campbell formed a society on the model of the early Methodist societies. His son Alexander now joined him from Scotland. He was a good scholar and a brilliant organiser. A genuine reluctance to divide the Christian Church still further made them hesitate to form a new denomination. And as, by 1812, father and son had become convinced of the unscriptural character of infant baptism, they made an association with the Baptists. This was to last only to 1832 when the Campbells and their friends became convinced that they must separate. Thus began a new communion of churches known, in America, as 'Disciples of Christ'. It is by far the largest indigenous religious group of worshippers in the United States today, and has a membership of nearly two million.

The origins of Churches of Christ in Great Britain are more complex. The early Glasites, as likewise their successors, stressed the importance of both intellect and emotions in the Christian life. Michael Faraday, the scientist, was one of them. No group of Christians has taken to heart more seriously the words of the Sarum Primer, 'God be in my head, and in my understanding'. Conversion has always been conceived as of the whole man. Excessive emotional ebullitions have never found favour. Like Gibbon, they deplore mistaking the giddiness of the head for the illumination of the spirit. Archibald McLean (1733–1812) was a learned Glasite who came to renounce paedobaptist views, and who helped to form a Scotch Baptist Church in Edinburgh, in 1765. It is from the Scotch (McLeanist) Baptists that the British Churches of Christ are in the main derived.

Churches of Christ seem always to have attracted serious Bible students. At one time it was no unusual thing for at least one-third of a congregation to read the Greek New Testament. This was the direct consequence of their conviction that the New Testament was the living Word of God, produced and preserved within a living society—the Church, out of a living experience. The New Testament is their ultimate authority in religion. But it is an authority set within a living institution which has the responsibility of interpretation. The Church is the Divine Society. 'It is as important', says Professor Lowber, 'to obey the bride as the bridegroom.'

It is a High Church doctrine. Indeed, it may be said that these nineteenth-century Protestants rediscovered the Church. For they hold the Church to be an objective, visible society, and entirely reject the idea of an invisible Church. Hence their conviction that all Christians should be united in one body, not in some kind of federation, but in organic union. Churches of Christ have never put forward the claim to be the *only* Churches of Christ. They are Churches of Christ only, and have assumed no sectarian names.

But if the object of the Movement is the Reunion of Christendom the means whereby this is to be accomplished is the restoration of the Body of Christ to a primitive purity, the 'Restoration of the Ancient Order of Things', as Alexander Campbell called it. A clear distinction is drawn between 'the Faith', and theological elaborations of the Faith. It is explained that in the New Testament the Christian Faith has to do with facts of history, and not with abstract ideas. 'With us', wrote Alexander Campbell in *The Christian System* (1835), 'Revelation has nothing to do with opinions on abstract reasonings, for it is founded wholly and entirely upon facts. . . . We say that facts are stubborn things. They are things, not words.' Hence the gospel is the redemptive activity of God, culminating in the things which happened to Jesus of Nazareth, declaring Him to be both Lord and Christ, Saviour and Redeemer of Mankind.

Churches of Christ are not indifferent to theology, nor are they unorthodox. But they take exception to the creeds and confessions of the sixteenth and seventeenth centuries. It is not on a credal basis that they foresee the scattered forces of the Christian Church being brought together, but by a return to that essential Christianity found only within the Apostolic Church. The final court of appeal is ever the Mind of Christ revealed in the New Testament.

It is for a New Testament Christianity that Churches of Christ plead. Never have they been Sabbatarian, and Professor William Robinson notes with approval the movement within the Anglican Church for the removal of the Ten Commandments from the Liturgy (*What Churches of Christ Stand For*, p. 46). 'The first essential of Christian life', says Professor Robinson, 'is faith in Jesus Christ as a Person, and not the acceptance of a series of dogmas, many of them conditioned by most subtle metaphysics, often quite outworn.'

Churches of Christ believe the two Sacraments of Baptism and the Lord's Supper to be real channels of grace. Infant baptism they hold to be unscriptural, and in 1812 both Thomas and Alexander Campbell were baptised by immersion following a public confession of the Lordship of Christ. 'There is in the Apostolic teaching no separation between conversion and regeneration such as Infant Baptism makes necessary.' Faith and repentance are held to be necessary prerequisites to baptism, but conversion must be of the intellect and the will as well as of the emotions. It is customary in Churches of Christ for Peter's Confession to be made audibly, before witnesses, by every candidate for baptism. Wholeheartedly is the affirmation of the Nicene Creed accepted, 'We believe in one Baptism for the remission of sins'. Baptism translates a man into a new relationship to the Godhead, changes his state, and introduces him into the sphere of grace—the Divine Society.

Churches of Christ strenuously resist any form of sacerdotalism. It is the Church which is the priestly body. Ministers, whether they be Presbyters, Deacons or Evangelists, do not style themselves 'reverend'. Some, but not all, are supported by stipends. It is the Church that is the priestly Israel of God, and it is Christ Himself who ordains, baptises, and dispenses the Supper.

From the early beginnings of the Movement it was recognised that the Christian religion, as found in the New Testament, is sacramental in principle. In 1843 Alexander Campbell could say that the most characteristic feature of the Movement was 'a restoration of the ordinances (i.e. Sacraments) to their place and power'. His followers were roundly accused of being Papists! This was absurd. They held no doctrines of transubstantiation or consubstantiation. But theirs was not a mere memorialism. They claimed that the Christian religion was one of 'positive institutions'. 'A "positive institution" was for them something done in the realm of reality and in the realm of personal action. It was a point at which the real action of God became sealed in our response, and in which the believer himself, ethically responding, became partaker of the Divine action' (*The Shattered Cross*, p. 86). John Glas had declared that the Lord's Supper should be the centre of worship on the Lord's Day, and the Eucharist as a corporate act of worship for the whole Christian community has always been essential teaching and practice in this communion. It is interesting to observe that this recognition of the Lord's Supper as the central act of worship anticipated by many years the Catholic revival in the Church of England. The eighteenth-century Glasites rejected that over-emphasis on preaching to which the Presbyterianism of the period was prone. In Great Britain the Lord's Table, and not the pulpit, occupied the central position in a church.

Celebrations are noteworthy for their sincerity and simplicity. There is a minimum of ritual, and no vestments. But they are remarkable in three ways. In the first place they are presided over by a President whose duty it is to serve the Communion from behind a table to the servers. The President is usually an ordained minister. But he is not regarded as the Celebrant. The true Celebrant at Holy Communion is Christ Himself. The individual minister does not stand in the place of Christ. His function is only to preside.

In the second place the active participation of the laity is encouraged. Churches of Christ have witnessed to what they call 'mutual ministry'. This is the right of all laymen who are duly qualified and gifted to read, pray, and preach at Divine Worship. Protestantism is committed to the priesthood of all believers. But in actual practice the conduct of services is almost entirely in the hands of the ministry. Churches of Christ have endeavoured to encourage a more active co-operation during 'the Prayers of the Church'. Every Communion Service includes 'The Prayers of the Brethren' when any member of the congregation is free to lead in prayer. It has been the experience of this communion that their celebrations are enriched in this way. They are not unaware of the difficulties involved, but it would seem that the ministers train their people in the proper observance of so solemn a privilege. This is not without very great interest for an age that has seen the introduction of the Dialogue Mass in the Church of Rome. Pius X defined the objective of liturgical reform as the 'active participation of the faithful in the Sacred Mysteries and in the solemn public prayer of the Church'. Always have Churches of Christ stressed the need of 'active participation of the faithful' at the Eucharist.

In the third place Churches of Christ have given much thought to the improvement of the lectionary. Formerly lessons from the Old and New Testaments for the weekly Communion Service were prepared a year at a time. But in 1952 a four-year cycle of lessons was issued, consisting of an Old Testament lesson, and two New Testament lessons, one an Epistle, the other a Gospel. Special lessons were also designed for special occasions. The new lectionary introduces an innovation. Each lesson is provided with a brief 'title' or 'heading' designed to focus the thought of the passage, and to link the three lessons together either in similarity or in contrast. It is suggested that they should be used at the beginning of each lesson. These headings were prepared by Mr. James Gray, M.A., of Leicester, who was associated with Professor William Robinson and Principal A. L. Brown of Overdale College, Birmingham, in the drawing up of the lectionary.

Thus for 30th June 1963 the lessons appointed are:

Lesson	*Title*
Genesis xxii, 1–19	God will provide for Himself the lamb.
Romans viii, 31–9	God spared not His own Son.
John iii, 16–21	He sent His Son that the world should be saved through Him.

The Council Fathers at the Vatican are considering a three- or even four-year cycle of Bible passages to enable the Scriptures to play a greater part in the Liturgy of the Mass. Father Hermann Schmidt, S.J., Professor of Liturgy at the Gregorian University, has emphasised that it is the pope's own wish that the Bible and the Chalice should be at the heart of Christian living. The Liturgical Movement is pervasive.

Momentous though this may be it must not be forgotten that the compilers of King Edward's Book anticipated by some centuries the Liturgical Reform Movement in the Church of Rome. It was they who recovered the conception of worship as an act of common prayer. It was they who decided that the public services of the Church should be in the vernacular. Moreover it was they who made provision for a systematic liturgical reading of the Bible. They deplored that 'these many years passed, this godly and decent order of the ancient Fathers hath been so altered, broken, and neglected, by planting in uncertain stories, legends, responds, verses, vain repetitions, commemorations, and synodals, that commonly when any book of the Bible was begun, before three or four chapters were read out, all the rest were unread.' Churches of Christ are the heirs, consciously or unconsciously, of the Prayer Book tradition.

Churches of Christ may be only a small group of churches as far as this country is concerned. But their real intellectuality and deep earnestness of purpose command respect. The entire Ecumenical Movement is in their debt.

PART III

The Heterodox Tradition

CHAPTER X

THE NEW CHURCH
(Swedenborgian)

THE New Church is considered to be the Christian Church reborn. It is not regarded by adherents as a sect. Rather they believe it to be Christianity transfigured. 'Ye must be born again', said Christ to Nicodemus. Spiritual rebirth is the essential condition for human salvation. Only so can man born of woman become a 'new man'. The New Church is the Church of the 'new man'. It was revealed to St. John the Divine. 'And I John saw the holy city, new Jerusalem, coming down from God out of heaven, prepared as a bride adorned for her husband.' For centuries the old Church survived, only to die of its own corruptions. The New Church, which is the New Jerusalem, came into being at the Second Advent. Already has Christ come again. The Lord's second coming and the last judgment are spiritual events that have taken place. Failure to realise this is common because His Second Advent is not in Person but in the power and glory of the Spirit of Truth. Under Providence, Emanuel Swedenborg has testified to these things.

To speak of Swedenborg as the founder of the New Church is to commit an obvious solecism. Swedenborg but revealed what had taken place. The Christian Church had been reborn. It is not surprising that Swedenborg founded no sect of his own. It was not until his death that churches came into being to protect and promulgate his teaching. In common parlance these churches were called 'Swedenborgian'. It was not a name to despise.

Emanuel Swedenborg, the son of a Lutheran bishop, was born in Stockholm in 1688. After an extensive education at Uppsala, London, Paris and Utrecht he was appointed by Charles XII of Sweden assessor-extraordinary in the Royal College of Mines. His skill in practical engineering was in evidence at the siege of Friedrichshall when he invented machines for transporting boats over land. It was still possible in the eighteenth century for a man of genius to acquire encyclopaedic knowledge. Swedenborg's intellectual achievements were of almost unbelievable dimensions. He became an expert in metallurgy. His work on palaeontology made him the predecessor of all Scandinavian geologists. He appears to have anticipated Kant and Laplace in his nebular hypothesis theory of the formation of the planets. He is credited by the French chemist Dumas with the first attempt to establish a system of crystallography. He was the first to employ mercury for the air pump. He devised a method of determining longitude at sea by observations of the moon among the stars. Perhaps his most extraordinary achievements were in physiological science, particularly with regard to the functions of the brain. Later in life Swedenborg declared that the Lord had introduced him first to the natural sciences as preparation for illumination.

It was in 1745 that the sight of his spirit was opened to see the heavens and the hells. In his *Arcana Coelestia* (1749) he wrote: 'It is expedient here to premise, that, of the Lord's Divine mercy, it has been granted me, now for several years, to be constantly and uninterruptedly in company with spirits and angels, hearing them converse with each other, and conversing with them. Hence it has been permitted me to hear and see things in another life which are astonishing, and which have never before come to the knowledge of any man, nor entered into his imagination. I have there been instructed concerning different kinds of spirits, and the state of souls after death—concerning hell, or the lamentable state of the unfaithful—and particularly concerning the doctrine of faith which is acknowledged throughout all heaven.' With this statement the scientist becomes the seer, or, as Emerson says of him in a famous essay, 'the last Father in the Church'.

Swedenborgians accept this claim. Others find it indefensible. No one has ever doubted the writer's good faith. Swedenborg was of great modesty and gentle bearing. His intellectual powers remained undiminished to the end. He exercised an important influence on Elizabeth Barrett, and on Browning himself. For some time William Blake was a member of the New Jerusalem Church, and his most famous song is of Jerusalem in England's green and pleasant land. Coleridge, Balzac and Henry James, the philosopher, were students of Swedenborg. Of recent years the Spiritualists have claimed him as one of their own, but Swedenborgians will have none of this. It remains that well-authenticated stories of supersensory experience have still to be explained in some way. One of the most famous is of Swedenborg's kindly offices for a poor widow who was harried by a tradesman to pay a bill already settled. Swedenborg consulted the dead husband. And the receipt was discovered in a concealed drawer in his bureau. Swedenborg must remain a mystery for all but his followers. But who can doubt the validity of the style on the title-page of his books, 'Servant of the Lord Jesus Christ'? Swedenborg died in London in 1772. In 1908 his remains were removed to Uppsala, at the request of the Swedish government, to find a final resting-place in the Cathedral.

Swedenborg claims to have received revelation from the Lord. 'Our Saviour visibly revealed Himself before me, and commanded me to do what I have done.' Therefore his teachings are authoritative. New Church liturgies endorse this view. Thus in a Catechism for Children included in the 1831 liturgy this answer is given to the question, 'Where can you gain further instruction?' 'In the writings of the Lord's servant, Emanuel Swedenborg; who was appointed by him to communicate information to mankind on these important subjects.'

Swedenborg's writings are voluminous. They include *Arcana Coelestia*, *The True Christian Religion*, *The Apocalypse Explained*, and *Heaven and Hell*. His doctrines may be summarised as follows. God is One both in essence and in person. The Divine Person is the Lord Jesus Christ. Jesus is Jehovah manifested in the finite garment of humanity. He was and is, 'Alpha and Omega, the Beginning and the End, the First and the Last, Who is and Who was, and Who is to come, the Almighty.'

God from eternity, the one Divine Being, embraces in Himself a trinity of Father, Son, and Holy Spirit. As in every human being there is a trinity of soul and body, and an operation of these together, so in the Lord there is a divine trinity. The Father is divine love and good. The Son is divine wisdom and truth. The Holy Spirit is love and wisdom proceeding from the Divine Humanity of the Lord. The Father was in Jesus, as the soul of a man is in his body. The Divine Person is God-Man, or as Swedenborg says, 'God is a Man'. The heart of the Cosmic God is human.

Swedenborg repudiates the conception of a vicarious Atonement. Jesus died for us, not instead of us. There is no question of reconciling God with man. The need is for man to be reconciled with God. 'God is mercy itself and pity itself, because He is love itself and goodness itself. It is a contradiction to say that mercy itself or goodness itself can look on a man with anger, and decide his own destruction, and still retain its own essence. Such things can hardly be attributed to an upright man or an angel in heaven, but rather to a wicked man or an infernal spirit. But if we inquire into the cause of this we shall trace it to the fact that men have mistaken the passion on the cross for redemption itself: hence have flowed those ideas as a series of false conclusions flow from one false principle. From a cask of vinegar nothing but vinegar can come forth' (*True Christian Religion*). It is important to clarify here a matter of some difficulty. Sometimes it is stated that the New Church is Patripassianist. But this is denied by New Church theologians. They maintain that the 'Lord suffered not as to His Divine, but as to His Human'. God the Father did not, and could not suffer. That which suffered in the Lord was the humanity derived from Mary. As the Lord was suffering He was not conscious of the indwelling Divine. He became conscious of His Divinity only when His sufferings ceased. His inmost soul, which was the Father, was beyond contact with suffering or evil. The Lord having suffered as a man, and triumphed over His sufferings, the door was opened to an awareness of Who and What He was essentially—God in the Flesh.

Swedenborg accepts the Holy Scriptures as the revelation of God. But he anticipates many modern thinkers in holding that the Bible is of unequal value. Only the books of the highest spiritual value constitute the Word. Such writings are of a distinctive character, being expressed in the symbolic language of parable, metaphor, and 'correspondence'. 'Correspondence' denotes here a relation between the things of earth and heaven. Thus the spiritual sense of the sixth commandment, 'Thou shalt not kill', means that thou shalt not destroy the souls of men by any evil influence; and the celestial sense means that thou shalt not hate the Lord. Swedenborg's discovery of allegorical meanings is reminiscent of the mediaeval Schoolmen. It will be seen that the New Church has a new canon. For the Word consists only of Genesis; Exodus; Leviticus; Numbers; Deuteronomy; Joshua; Judges; Samuel, I and II; Kings, I and II; Psalms; the Prophets from Isaiah to Malachi; the four Gospels; the Apocalypse. The rest of the Bible is held in respect. Though not part of the Word, Swedenborg valued the Epistles highly.

Swedenborg makes the extraordinary assertion that he witnessed the Last Judgment in 1757. 'It has been granted me to see with my own eyes that the Last Judgment is now accomplished.' Evil spirits, the souls of wicked men, were attempting to destroy all spiritual life on the Earth. Only the intervention of God leashed these diabolical beings, and made possible an influx of new spiritual forces among men. The progress of the world since that time is the direct outcome of this judgment. And Christ has come again. Not this time is the Word made flesh. But His Second Coming is in the spirit, a revelation of the inner glory of the Divine Word. Of this Second Advent Swedenborg is himself the instrument. Through him is revealed the spiritual sense of the Divine Word illuminating Holy Writ.

Swedenborg propounds a Way of Salvation. He rejects justification by faith. 'God is never angry. He condemns no one to hell, but leads all, if only they will follow, to heaven.' It will be observed that Swedenborg has something in common here with Dante. But he goes on to assert that it is the Divine purpose that men should become angels, for all angels were formerly men. Heaven and Hell are states of mind. Not even good works as such can save a soul. Swedenborg tells how, in the spiritual world, he encountered some Socinians sinking to hell. They were so proud of their noble characters! A detailed panorama of the life after death is to be found in the book *Heaven and Hell*. It would appear that hell exists because it is so popular. Men and women of evil heart tend to congregate there. They would feel diffident in heaven. Although there is no personal Devil, people become, in their future existence, what at heart they really are—devils or angels. And for the Lord Himself the blessed angels will appear before Him like one man in singleness of heart. This is the *maximus homo* of Swedenborg. His 'Grand

Man' is like to a great orchestra in which each does his part to the glory of the whole.

Swedenborg made no attempt to found an ecclesiastical society. He believed that members of all churches could belong to the New Church. For the true Church is invisible and indestructible. It is constituted by a genuine love of truth and goodness, and by a spiritual relation established with the Lord in the minds of men. But followers of Swedenborg found themselves in a dilemma. Many found it difficult to worship in harmony with members of other communions, whose beliefs appeared to them insufficient. Hence came into being the society of churches known as the New Jerusalem Church, or the New Church. But there have always been many nonseparatist Swedenborgians. The Rev. John Clowes, rector of St. John's Church, Manchester, was the great apostle of Swedenborg in Lancashire. But he made an especial journey to London to remonstrate with his friends who contemplated secession from the Establishment. Hindmarsh, in his *Rise and Progress of the New Church*, says that Clowes 'thought it probable, that sooner or later the bishops and other dignitaries of the Church of England would be disposed to revise their Liturgy, and make it conformable to the truths of the new dispensation'. Other Swedenborgians were less sanguine. Among these was Robert Hindmarsh, Printer Extraordinary to the Prince of Wales. With a small group of friends this enthusiastic disciple held weekly meetings in the Inner Temple for the study of Swedenborg's doctrines. The outcome of these conferences was the formation, in 1784, of 'The Theosophical Society, instituted for the purpose of promoting the Heavenly Doctrines of the New Jerusalem, by translating, printing, and publishing the Theological Writings of Emanuel Swedenborg.' Among the members was the celebrated sculptor, John Flaxman. One of the interesting features of Swedenborgian societies has been a tireless propaganda. Swedenborg was himself a great believer in the power of the press, and the Swedenborg Society, which is independent of the New Church, has followed his example since 1810.

The formal organisation of the New Church came into being in 1787. Robert Hindmarsh inaugurated the meeting. The first church for public worship was opened in Eastcheap,

London, in 1788. There are today some seventy churches in Britain. The New Church is strong in Lancashire. There the influence of John Clowes, described by de Quincey as 'Holiest of men whom it has been my lot to meet', still persists. The church in Accrington has been described as a 'Swedenborgian cathedral'. Other churches are to be found in Sweden, Switzerland, Germany, Italy, and in the European countries generally. Flourishing churches exist in Canada, the United States and in Australasia. There are small groups in the Far East. A large mission exists in South Africa, and a smaller one in West Africa. Numerically, the New Church is most considerable in America.

It would appear that the early members of the New Church found it difficult to frame an order of worship. This was due to the eclectic character of the congregations. Robert Hindmarsh, in a preface to one of the eighteenth-century liturgies, wrote: 'While some have judged, that the forms to be adopted should, in their external appearance and phraseology, resemble as much as possible those of the old establishments, and yet remain free from the gross errors of doctrine now so prevalent in them all; others have been of opinion, that the service of the New Church should bear as little affinity, in any shape, to that of the Old Church, as the nature of public worship will permit.' Some of the early societies of the New Church conducted public worship according to no prescribed form. They fancied extemporaneous prayers and praise. But Hindmarsh advocated liturgical worship. Since his time, at least fifteen liturgies have appeared, some running into many editions. Before the end of the eighteenth century, three distinct liturgies were forthcoming, Robert Hindmarsh's *Liturgy of the New Church* being printed in at least five editions.

As with any federation of churches organised on a congregational basis, much variety of practice has persisted. As early as 1800, the York Street Chapel in St. James's Square, Westminster, published a prayer book of its own. Other books were issued for congregations at Bolton Street, Salford (1813); St. George's Chapel, near Oldham Road, Manchester (1819); Islington (1858); and Argyle Square Church, King's Cross, London (1859, 1863). But New Church authorities were anxious to introduce a common liturgy. The influential *Liturgy of the*

New Church, signified by the New Jerusalem, in the Revelation, first published in 1802, was the work of a number of ministers. In 1807, *Rites and Ceremonies for the use of the Lord's Church* was drawn up by a conference of the London churches and recommended to the Provinces. One of the ministers responsible for this Order was Joseph Proud, a famous preacher, and a friend of Joseph Priestley. In 1828 a liturgy was prepared by order of the General Conference. In a lengthy preface it is stated that 'most of the congregations have preferred the use of a Liturgy: others, however, have always conducted all the parts of their public services in the extemporary manner. But societies having sprung up in various parts of the kingdom, having, at first, little communication with each other, various Liturgies have been brought into use. It has, therefore, long been deemed an object of considerable importance by the General Conference, to establish, for those societies which prefer the use of a form, one general Liturgy.' The General Conference recommended their liturgy. But no attempt was made to impose it on non-liturgical congregations.

Many of the liturgies are derived from previous productions. Thus the two editions of *The Liturgy of the New Church, with the Rites and Ceremonies*, London, 1810, are almost identical with the two editions of *The Liturgy of the New Church, signified by the New Jerusalem, in the Revelation*, London, 1802, 1805. Again, the two services for morning and evening in *The Liturgy of the New Church* (1828) prepared by order of the General Conference appear in the subsequent liturgies authorised by the Conference in 1875, 1903, 1912 and (with amendments) 1925. Eight additional services included in the 1875 edition of *Liturgy for the New Church* are printed in the editions of 1903, 1912 and (with amendments) 1925. Two responsive services introduced into the 1903 edition of *Liturgy for the New Church* are reproduced in the editions of 1912 and (with amendments) 1925. The 1903 edition contains Morning and Evening Services from the Prayer Book. This was reprinted in 1912 but not in 1925. A Litany and a responsive service of Thanksgiving for occasional use included in the 1875 book were incorporated in the books of 1903, 1912 and (with amendments) 1925. It is interesting to note that the 1925 book includes services for Christmas Day, Easter Day and Whit Sunday.

New Church liturgies may be divided into two categories, original compositions and revisions of the Prayer Book.

The most notable feature of the original compositions is their heavily doctrinal emphasis. Although Swedenborg's name appears only in the services of the oldest liturgy (1790, 1791), his teaching is fundamental. The original prayers avoid much of the verbosity of the eighteenth century, though couched in the quaint language of the period. Such is the following prayer from *The Liturgy of the New Church* (1790). 'Adorable Lord Jesus, who in these latter days hast been graciously pleased to manifest thyself a second time unto the children of men, in the power and glory of thy holy Word, by revealing the spiritual and celestial senses thereof, wherein thou hast thy most immediate residence, and by the light of which proceeding from thy Divine Humanity, we are enabled through mercy to approach thee alone as our Father and our God, our Creator, Redeemer, and Regenerator; we pray for the prosperity of thy New Jerusalem Church, now descending from thee out of heaven.'

It is noticeable that the New Church conformed to the Anglican norm of the period. Thus the 1790 liturgy provides orders for morning and evening prayer, with an order of the Holy Supper as an additional and occasional service. The following is the order of morning service taken from the 1828 liturgy the first to be authorised by the General Conference:

> Hymn (*all standing*)
> Sentences of the Word
> Invitation to Worship
> Confession (*all kneeling*)
> The Lord's Prayer
> Prayer for Blessing on Reading of the Word
> Old Testament Lesson
> Doxology
> Chant
> Portion of the Psalms (*read by Minister*)
> Doxology
> New Testament Lesson
> Doxology
> The Decalogue (*read by the Minister. All standing*)

149

Hymn
Prayers for Various Blessings and Benefits
Prayers of Thankgsiving
Benediction
Hymn (*the Minister ascends the Pulpit*)
Short Prayer
Sermon
Hymn
Short Prayer
Benediction

The Prayer Book has found a new home in the New Church. The earliest liturgy printed by R. Hindmarsh in 1790 shows traces of this influence. Morning service includes a Prayer for the King, a Prayer for all Conditions of Men, and a General Thanksgiving. All these are revised. Most interesting is the prayer in evening service for the Bishops, Priests and Ministers of the Old Church.

It was in 1793 that a liturgy was devised, expressly based on the Prayer Book. This was *The Liturgy of the Lord's New Church (signified by the New Jerusalem in the Revelation), formed upon the plan of that of the Church of England*. The preface deplores the erroneous ideas of the Establishment, 'respecting the Christian Redeemer, and salvation by "Faith Alone".' But the editor acknowledges great merit in the Church of England. 'It is no less certain, that, acknowledging the divinity of Jesus Christ, and the necessity of a life according to the precepts of the Decalogue, she addresseth many of her prayers expressly to the Lord God the Saviour, and hath judiciously made the Commandments a part of her Morning Service. And by reading out of the Word of God, on her days of public worship, lessons, psalms, and select portions from the gospels, which, from the highest authority, remind her congregations from time to time of the general dispensations of an all-ruling Providence, of the particular duties invariably required of all men, and of the astonishing mercies successively vouchsafed by the Lord during the state of our redemption: in these particulars, she appears to have considerably the advantage over those other denominations of professing Christians, who, confining their religious worship to the singing of hymns, extempore prayer and preaching, quote only such texts of Scripture as seem to themselves more strongly to corroborate their own favourite doctrines and tenets.' It would seem that the framers of the liturgy also saw an advantage in a revision of a book so well known as the Anglican. A comparison could not fail to draw special attention to both common and peculiar tenets.

The liturgy published in 1802 is likewise a Prayer Book revision. It was reprinted in 1805. The liturgy of 1810 is almost identical with it.

In 1891 appeared *An Outline of the Form of Worship used in St. George's Chapel, near Oldham Road, Manchester.* This is a Prayer Book revision.

No other revision appears until 1903. The liturgy of that year includes *Morning and Evening Services from the Book of Common Prayer revised for the use of the New Church.* It was reissued in 1912.

Analysis of Prayer Book Revisions

RITES AND CEREMONIES

All New Church societies now adhere to the liturgical form. Congregations are supposed to kneel for prayer, though this is not always observed. Ministers wear cassock and surplice for the entire service. The academic hood is worn occasionally. The distinctive feature of New Church vestments is the stole. The ordaining ministers, who are in fact the bishops, wear red stoles, the older ministers blue or purple stoles, while young ministers but newly ordained wear green stoles. This is in keeping with Swedenborg's teaching as to the significance of colours.

A copy of the Word always stands on the altar table. This is opened at the beginning of the service by the minister, with the congregation standing. It is closed at the end. It is held that the entire service is, in spirit, an opening of the Word.

MORNING PRAYER

The word 'minister' is used in these liturgies. But the word 'priest' is employed in the Ordination service in the 1807 Rites and Ceremonies. It is used as an alternative to 'minister', nor is any other significance to be suspected! Scripture lessons are read from the Word alone. The New Church Calendar is composed only of those genuine 'Books of the Word, which contain the internal sense' (Preface: 1790 *Liturgy*). Thus the Epistles are not read in public worship. All prayers are addressed to Jesus. It is interesting to observe that Swedenborgians, in the time-honoured manner of Christians, have adapted well-known hymns. Thus a verse in the 1813 hymnal reads,

Jesus, our help in ages past,
Our hope for years to come.

The New Church liturgies change the first words of the General Confession to: 'Almighty and most merciful Lord' (1793); 'Almighty and most merciful Jehovah-Jesus' (1802); and 'O Lord Jesus Christ, our heavenly Father; we have erred, and strayed from Thy ways like lost sheep' (1903). The words, 'for his sake' are deleted. The Absolution is omitted from the 1793 and 1802 liturgies. 'A Prayer for the Remission of Sins, to be pronounced by the Minister, the people still kneeling', is included in the 1903 book. It is the Anglican Absolution save that it begins, 'O Lord Jesus Christ, who desirest not the death of a sinner', with the omissions of 'through Jesus Christ our Lord', and 'hath given power, and commandment to his Ministers', etc. The versicles after the Lord's Prayer are retained only in the 1903 book. The *Gloria Patri* is omitted, and replaced by 'To Jesus Christ be glory and dominion for ever and ever'. A very free rendering of the Te Deum is given in the St. George's Chapel (1819) liturgy. The 1903 version is very close to the original, but the following changes are made. The words 'Thine honourable, true, and only Son' become 'The honourable, true, and only Son'. Again, 'Thou art the everlasting Son of the Father' becomes 'Thou art the everlasting God and our Father'. 'Thou sittest at the right hand of God' becomes 'Thou sittest at the right hand of Power'. Very significant is the change from 'We believe that thou shalt come to be our Judge', to 'We believe that Thou O Lord wilt be our Judge'. Jesus Christ has come. The Benedicite is omitted. So is the Apostles' Creed. The versicles that follow the creed succeed the Ten Commandments in the 1903 book. The collect for Peace is adapted in the 1793 and 1903 books. In the latter it begins: 'O Lord Jesus Christ, Who art the author of peace', and ends 'may not fear the power of any adversaries, O Saviour of the world'. The collect for Grace in the 1903 book omits 'through Jesus Christ our Lord'. A very free rendering of the Prayer for the King's Majesty appears in the 1790 and 1802 books. The prayers in the 1903 book for the King and the Royal Family follow the Prayer Book, save that the prayer for the King begins: 'O Lord Jesus Christ, our heavenly Father, high and mighty, King of Kings'. As usual, 'through Jesus Christ our Lord', is removed. The 1793 book includes the Bishops with the ministers in the Prayer for the Clergy and People (evening service). The 1903 book reads, 'all Ministers'. The Prayer of St. Chrysostom is in the 1793 and 1903 books. The blessing in these New Church liturgies is usually, 'The grace of our Lord Jesus Christ be with you all. Amen.'

EVENING PRAYER

The changes are similar to those made in Morning Prayer.

QUICUNQUE VULT

This is omitted.

THE LITANY

Only one Litany in the New Church prayer books is based on the Book of Common Prayer. The 1793 liturgy omits the Invocations, but bishops, priests and deacons are still prayed for.

OCCASIONAL PRAYER AND COLLECTS

Many of these are retained by the liturgies. Especially is this true of the 1793 book which adheres closely to the Christian Year. 'A General Thanksgiving' and 'A Prayer for the High Court of Parliament' are included in the 1903 book.

NEW CHURCH OCCASIONAL SERVICES

ORDINATIONS

In 1803 a conference of London ministers and Church delegates made provision for the Ordination of ministers. Ordinations were to be in public at the usual time of divine worship.

It was agreed that the candidate must be versed in the Hebrew, Greek, and Latin languages, and should testify to his belief in the writings of Emanuel Swedenborg.

An Order for the Ordination of Ministers was drawn up. It declared that 'the ordination of Ministers or Priests is effected by the imposition of hands'. It provided that the ordaining priest should read the Consecration from the Word as follows, 'Jesus said unto his disciples, Peace be unto you. As the Father hath sent Me even so send I you. And when He had said this, He breathed on them, and said unto them, Receive ye the Holy Ghost.'

Most of the New Church liturgies contain Orders of Baptism, the Holy Supper, and occasional services. The liturgy for the New Church compiled by order of the General Conference and published in 1925 is by far the most compendious Book of Praise and Prayer ever adopted by Conference. It includes services for the Baptism of Children and Adults, a Marriage Service, a Burial Service, services for the introduction of Junior and Senior Members, and an order for use in visiting the sick. It is to be noted, however, that the service of Churching, to be found in the 1793 and 1813 books, is not included.

HOLY BAPTISM

Swedenborg recognised baptism as one of the two sacraments of the Christian Church. But he insisted that baptism, as a ceremonial act and sacramental form, cannot save. It is but the beginning of a process that can lead to heaven by a good life well begun. As the 1903 liturgy declares: 'The first use of Baptism is, that a person may have the name of Christian, and be kept by angels, as the Lord's ministers, in a capacity of becoming what that name implies. The second is, that he may know by instruction that the Lord Jesus Christ is the Only God of heaven and earth, the Redeemer, Regenerator, and Saviour. The third use of Baptism is, that, by living according to the Divine Commandments, he may be regenerated by the Lord, and thus be redeemed and saved.' Thus the water used in baptism is a symbol of the truth that cleanses from sin. Truth is spiritual water. Swedenborg taught that angelic assistance is pledged to the furtherance of the baptismal effort. He further taught that all children who die, baptised or unbaptised, are given to the care of the wisest angels for their spiritual education. It should be noted that, although Swedenborg insisted on the exclusive divinity of Jesus, he did not believe that salvation was limited to professing Christians. In his own day he shocked his friends by saying that even noble Mahometans could be saved! The usual baptismal formula in these liturgies is 'I baptise thee into the Name of the Father, and of the Son, and of the Holy Spirit.' 'The New Church considers it unnecessary to have Godfathers and Godmothers. The Lord alone is the Father of all who are regenerated' (1790 *Liturgy*).

THE HOLY SUPPER

Swedenborg acknowledged this to be the Second Sacrament. In the Holy Supper our Lord is spiritually present. This is not due to any change in the elements, or any manner of administration. The sacredness of the Supper consists in the purely spiritual and divine things that are represented and expressed. The bread and the wine signify the flesh and the blood. By His flesh is meant every expression of His love, and by His blood, all truth. In the words of the 1813 liturgy: 'Since, therefore, the holy supper includes and contains in it the Lord, his divine good, and his divine truth, it follows that it also includes and contains, both universally and particularly, all things relating to heaven and the church. And whereas the Lord's flesh signifies the divine good of his love, and his blood the divine truth of his wisdom, it is evident that the Lord is completely omnipresent in the holy supper, both as to his Divinity and as to his Glorified Humanity. Thus eating and drinking are acts of a spiritual nature; and thus the holy supper becomes a signing, sealing, certifying, and witnessing, even before the angels, that the worthy receivers thereof are the sons of God.'

MARRIAGE

Swedenborg taught that true 'conjugal' love, which can only exist between one husband and one wife, is a primary charac-

155

teristic of the New Church. For it is grounded in the marriage of good and truth, and corresponds with the marriage of the Lord and His Church. It is more celestial than any other love in men or angels. Married partners, truly united in this world, will continue the same fellowship in the next. Sex is persistent, because in essence it is spiritual. Thus in the Marriage Service of the 1925 book it is declared: 'We are taught by the doctrines of the New Church that true marriage is the spiritual and heavenly union of two minds.'

BURIAL OF THE DEAD

No statement of Swedenborg's is so famous as this sentence from *Heaven and Hell*: 'Those who are in heaven are continually advancing to the springtime of life, and the more thousands of years they live, the more delightful is the spring to which they attain.' In the order included in the Rites and Ceremonies (1803), the commendation from the Prayer Book is changed to: 'Forasmuch as it hath pleased our heavenly Father, of his great mercy, to take out of the natural into the spiritual world, the soul of our dear brother here departed; we therefore commit his body to the ground, earth to earth, ashes to ashes, dust to dust, in humble hope of his attaining to the resurrection of eternal life in a spiritual world, the soul being the man in substance and form spiritual, and therefore the subject of that world immediately after death. So that our departed brother is not dead, but alive in that state and world to which we are all hastening; and having laid aside this mortal body, never more to reassume it, he there lives for ever in human form and substance.'

American liturgies consulted by the writer do not reveal any fundamental divergence from those already examined. The teaching of Swedenborg gives to them all a characteristic genre. But there is variety of expression in America, as in England. This may be seen by a comparison of *A Liturgy for the General Church of the New Jerusalem*, published in Pennsylvania in 1904 with *A Prayer Book and Hymnal for the use of the New Church*, published in the same State in 1868.

The 1904 liturgy is an elaborate production containing a variety of Sunday services and occasional services. The Sunday services include many responses by the minister and people, as well as selections from the Psalter to be read by minister and people in alternate lines. Certain parts of these services are indicated in outline only. Readers acquainted with New England Congregationalism and Unitarianism will recognise a familiar form of service. Thus the Harvard University Hymn Book contains many 'Responsive Readings'.

Of all New Church liturgies the 1868 book approximates the most faithfully to the Catholic tradition. An introductory note explains the Christian Year. Proper lessons are appointed for our Lord's Nativity, Circumcision, and Epiphany, the Annunciation of the Virgin Mary, the Nativity of St. John the Baptist, the Twelve Apostles, the Holy Innocents, and All Saints. Lessons are also appointed for the first Sunday in Advent, Ash Wednesday, Palm Sunday, the six days of Holy Week, Easter Day, the Sunday after Easter, Ascension Day, the Sunday after Ascension, and Whit Sunday. An interesting addition is the 'Feast of the Holy City', to commemorate the Descent of the Holy Jerusalem out of Heaven from God. This is appointed for the first Sunday after Pentecost. The Order of Public Worship is based on Morning Prayer in the Prayer Book. Orders of Mattins and Vespers are included for daily use. In these offices the word 'priest' is used. An amended form of the Apostles' Creed begins: 'I believe in God, the Father Almighty, Maker of heaven and earth, even Jesus Christ our only Lord and Saviour.' A revised Anglican Litany is included, with invocations to 'Holy Lord God', 'Father in heaven', 'Redeemer of the world, Spirit of Truth and Comforter'. Any implication of Tri-Personalism is avoided. The most remarkable feature of the liturgy is the inclusion of Lauds and Compline for the use of schools and colleges.

PART IV

The Catholic Tradition

This short, concluding section may appear to be something of a curiosity in a book devoted to the Free Churches, and certainly the Catholic Apostolic Church and the Society of Free Catholics never made any serious impression on Free Church life. Nevertheless, they did arise (a thing remarkable in itself), and no survey would be complete without some reference to them, more especially in a liturgical study.

Of minor importance, perhaps, in themselves, they are not without a more profound significance. The Puritans were antipathetic to the ancient Catholic tradition, very largely because they thought of it in terms of Roman Catholicism. That is why the sign of the cross in Baptism, the observance of Saints' Days, and the very name 'Catholic' seemed sinister to them. Today, the powerful Free Churches are hagridden no longer by an ancient fear. Moreover the relations between the Free Churches and the Church of England are closer and more cordial than ever before. These are the changed circumstances that have permitted many Free Churchmen to assess anew the Catholic tradition, and to perceive that it need not be altogether abandoned because once upon a time it was suspect. One illuminating instance of this is the revival of the Christian Year in the Free Churches.

CHAPTER XI

THE CATHOLIC APOSTOLIC CHURCH

THE Church of Christ has long awaited the coming of her Lord. Throughout the Christian era men have turned from the confusion of their times to the promised millenium. 'And I saw an angel come down from heaven, having the key of the bottomless pit and a great chain in his hand. And he laid hold on the dragon, that old serpent, which is the Devil, and Satan, and bound him a thousand years' (Revelation xx, 2). Interest in millenarianism rose to a height in the period following Waterloo. The Apocalyptic tendencies of the age found expression in contemporary art and in Byron's *Heaven and Earth*. The Christian conscience had been shocked by the atheistical extravagances of the French Revolution. Parisian Jacobins had adored a pretty actress as goddess of Reason in the Cathedral of Notre-Dame. Afterwards had come the Napoleonic terror. To many it seemed that the last days were at hand.

In 1826 Henry Drummond, a banker of some wealth, began a series of conferences at his home, Albury Park, Surrey, for searchings of the Scriptures. Among those who attended were a future bishop and dean of the Church of England. But the most famous frequenter of this 'School of the Prophets' was Edward Irving, a clergyman of the Church of Scotland, remarkable for the charm and beauty of his preaching.

Edward Irving remains something of an enigma. A lover of the Church of Scotland, he was expelled from her ministry. Later renowned as leader of the 'Irvingites', he held only subordinate rank among them. His brilliance, his thwarted love-affair with Jane Welsh, afterwards Mrs. Thomas Carlyle, his chequered ecclesiastical career, and early death provided Mrs. Oliphant and other writers with romantic fact and fiction. Perhaps the truth was that his intellect was not the equal of his eloquence. Dr. Chalmers, whom he had assisted at St. John's Church, Glasgow, described the young man's preaching as 'Italian music'. But fashionable London flocked to hear him on his removal to the Caledonian Church, and his admirers included the statesman Canning. In 1827, the congregation moved from small, humble quarters in Hatton Garden to a new church in Regent Square. This ornate building, with a front that is a replica of York Minster, still stands. The year before, a book had been published by a Spanish Jesuit under the pseudonym of Ben Ezra, entitled *The Coming of the Messiah in Glory and Majesty*. It exercised a profound influence on Irving.

Meanwhile petitions were being offered to Heaven in prayer meetings for the outpouring of the Holy Spirit. The Rev. J. Haldane Stewart, a clergyman of the Church of England, published a tract on the promise in Joel, 'I will pour out my Spirit upon all flesh', which had a wide circulation both at home and on the Continent. Members of the Catholic Apostolic Church believe that the cry for the Holy Ghost was answered for the first time on 28th March 1830. A young woman in Scotland, Mary Campbell, a devout Presbyterian, not only recovered from consumption but began to speak in 'unknown tongues'. Soon the 'power' came upon two brothers and a sister named Macdonald, at Port Glasgow. During the year 1831 several persons, Anglicans, Presbyterians, and Dissenters, received the gift of spiritual utterance. The 'tongues' were mysterious, but the 'prophecies' proclaimed the speedy advent of Christ and the duty of the Church to prepare His way. These were accompanied by acts of spiritual healing. Soon the prophecies counselled the restoration of all the lost ministries of the Church. In 1833 the word of prophecy revealed that a solicitor named Cardale had been called to be the first of twelve apostles.

The authorities of the Church of Scotland became alarmed at the association of Edward Irving with the new movement. Already his views on the humanity of Christ had led to a charge of heresy. Ignoring the remonstrances of his friends, Irving welcomed the 'tongues' of a worshipper at Regent Square Church. 'I did rejoice with great joy that the bridal jewels of the Church had been found again.' Irving was removed from the ministry of the Church of Scotland in 1833, to his great grief. And, as the Church of Scotland had taken away all that it had given him, he was thankful to accept ordination at the hands of the apostles. Accordingly he was ordained to the episcopate, and set in charge of the church in Newman Street. Next year he died. It must be understood that at no time did he make claim to supernatural gifts. In all meekness he submitted to the authority of the apostles, which had now been restored. Carlyle says this of him: 'His was the freest, brotherliest, bravest human soul mine ever came in contact with. I call him, on the whole, the best man I have ever, after trial enough, found in this world.' Irving was buried in the crypt of Glasgow Cathedral. In the lancet window, above his grave, is the figure of John the Baptist, crying in the wilderness. Like the Forerunner, Irving was the prophetic voice. But he had no constructive genius. The real founders of the Catholic Apostolic Church were Drummond, Cardale and the other apostles.

No exclusive claim has been made to the title, 'Catholic Apostolic' by the Irvingites. It appears to have come into use through a State census. Adherents employ it as appropriate to the one body of Christ, of which they are a part. By July 1835, the college of apostles had been increased to twelve by revelation, and 'separated' to a special work of blessing. Supreme authority was invested in the apostles. In accordance with St. Paul's teaching in the Epistle to the Ephesians, 'And He gave some, apostles; and some, prophets; and some, evangelists; and some, pastors and teachers; for the perfecting of the saints, for the work of the ministry': the fourfold ministry of apostles, prophets, evangelists and pastors was completed. Every congregation was organised under an 'angel' or bishop, assisted by elders and deacons. The ministry was not professional, as many continued in their everyday employments.

The Catholic Apostolic Church proclaims the infallibility of the Scriptures, and accepts the creeds of the Universal Church. Candidates for baptism assent to the Apostles' Creed, which is recited in the daily worship, morning and evening. The Nicene Creed is included in the Sunday Eucharist. The Athanasian Creed is recited on the four great feasts of Christmas, Easter, Pentecost, and All Saints. No pronouncement has been made on the *filioque* clause in the Nicene Creed. The Church maintains that although the restored apostles have promulgated no novelties, they have given proper prominence and exposition to the Incarnation, as the centre-point of God's dealings with His creatures. Thus they believe that it was the Father's purpose from all eternity that His Son should be made man, and as man be the Head and Ruler of the creation. This was 'the eternal purpose which He purposed in Christ Jesus our Lord' (Eph. iii, 11). Had there been no Fall and no need of redemption, the Son of God would have become man. The divine purpose to give man the pre-eminency was challenged by the devil. This was the origin of sin. The devil introduced sin and death into the world. Not only was the Son's promised inheritance usurped, but the human nature He was to make His own was desecrated. Redemption was possible only because the Son took upon Himself the nature of fallen humanity by being born of the Virgin Mary. The death of Christ atoned for the sins of the world, and His ascension exalted mankind to an honour and dominion not known before. The first work of His exaltation was to send down the Holy Ghost to form His body, the Church. Through the descent of the Holy Ghost the apostles were endowed with the prophetic gift. Without their cognisance, a new apostle was chosen by God. It was St. Paul's endeavour to entreat the Church to persevere in her task of spiritual perfection so that the Bride of Christ might be worthy of her Lord. But the Church was not worthy. The Lord's return was postponed. The apostolic office was lost, not to be restored again till the nineteenth century.

It has been the especial duty of this group of Christians to bear final testimony to the Day of the Lord. In 1836 they acquainted the bishops of the Church of England with their revelation. Two years later the rulers of Church and State throughout Europe were presented with a testimony in which the evils of the time were traced to their spiritual source, the departure of the Church from God. Even the pope was informed. The emissaries of the Church who journeyed to the Continent became acquainted with Roman Catholic ritual and the supreme rite of the Mass. Hence arose that interest in liturgiology which culminated in 1842 in the publication of *The Liturgy and other Divine Offices of the Church*. 'It is undoubtedly', says Heiler, 'one of the finest and fullest forms of Christian worship. Indeed, of all the liturgies of today it comes perhaps nearest to the Primitive Church.' *The Liturgy* is based on Anglican, Roman and Greek rites. Services are enriched with lights, incense and vestments.

The Catholic Apostolic Church was introduced into Bavaria by William Caird in 1841, but its greatest extension has been in North Germany. Congregations are to be found in various parts of the world, but the Church has ceased to grow. This is because it has fulfilled its mission. The twelve apostles and their coadjutors have passed away. No ordinations have been possible since 1901, as only apostles could ordain. From that time onward minister after minister has died, and altar after altar has been 'covered'. But the faithful are not disheartened. Never have they regarded the Catholic Apostolic Church as a sect. Those who have been 'sealed' by the laying on of hands to bear witness to the coming of Christ await Him now in this 'period of silence'. Many are members of the Church of England. Anglican bishops are revered as successors of the 'angels' who presided over the apostolic churches at the beginning. Generous tributes have been forthcoming for a group of high-principled and spiritually-minded Christians who love the Church so well that they contribute tithes for her maintenance. The Anglican clergy find them excellent parishioners, and it is pleasing to recall that the last 'angel' of the stately church in Gordon Square was visited before his death by Dr. Winnington-Ingram, Bishop of London.

It was noticed by observers in the early days, how close was the resemblance between the 'Irvingite' and 'Puseyite' movements. Both Mr. Irving and Dr. Newman turned their backs on what the former called 'the serpent-cunning of the liberal spirit'. Each made the pilgrimage to what he believed to be the ancient Catholic Church, though Newman thought it existed still, and Irving saw it as newly risen from the dying embers of the past. Both held high views of the Christian ministry as a priesthood, and of the sacraments as real means of grace.

The Catholic Apostolic Church teaches the validity of two sacraments, Baptism and the Lord's Supper, in which there are both 'the outward, visible sign, and the inward spiritual grace'. Baptism is not deemed to be an indispensable essential to salvation, for those outside the Church, as this would be a limitation of God's power. It is believed that, after consecration, the elements of bread and wine in the Lord's Supper become spiritually and really the Body and Blood of Christ, though without change of substance. The restored apostles rejected transubstantiation, and repudiated the conception of the Eucharistic sacrifice as a repetition of the death of Christ. The Eucharist commemorates the sacrifice once made for all.

It should be noted that prayers for the departed do not imply any belief in purgatory. Saints' Days are not observed. Provision is made for private confession and absolution, but is neither compulsory nor inquisitorial. The rite of anointing the sick is intended for the healing of the body. Unlike the Roman Catholic sacrament of extreme unction it is not designed to prepare the soul for death. Meetings are held for extemporaneous prayer.

The liturgy of the Catholic Apostolic Church evolved under the guidance of the restored apostles. For two years after the 'separation' of 1835, ministers offered their own prayers in the Presbyterian manner. The apostles then issued a lithographed form of Communion Service. In 1842 a liturgy of a tentative nature, and for use only at Albury, was printed. It was not sent out to the churches. In 1843 the first edition of the *Liturgy* for churches was issued. New editions were forthcoming in 1847, 1851, 1853, 1856, 1863, 1869 and 1880. There have thus been in all eight editions, with additions in each. Reprints only have been published since 1880.

An important feature of the 1843 edition was the new service for All Saints' Day. In the Communion Service for that day the Athanasian Creed was printed in two columns in both English and Latin. It appears that the restored apostles did not approve fully of the English translation. The order for the administration of Holy Communion did not occupy a first place in the 1843 book. The apostles had yet to recognise this order as the principal service of Christian worship. Communion was still administered to the people sitting in their seats, as in the Scottish Church. With this edition, vestments were introduced.

The Holy Communion office was called for the first time the Holy Eucharist in the 1847 edition. Not yet was it placed at the beginning of the book.

The Holy Eucharist was inserted at the beginning of the

1851 edition. Forms for Ordination were introduced. Lights and incense came into use in 1852.

The form for the consecration of chrism was introduced into the 1856 edition, and in the 1869 edition a form for the blessing of holy water.

Four editions of the *Liturgy* were issued for Scotland in 1848, 1849, and 1861–3 under the direction of the apostle Drummond. But in 1870 the English *Liturgy* was substituted. An edition was issued for Canada in 1848. The *Liturgy* has been translated into eleven languages.

Never has a Burial Service been included in the book. At the date of its compilation burials in England were conducted by the Anglican clergy. The apostle Drummond issued a Burial Service for Scotland almost identical with the Anglican.

The influence of the Book of Common Prayer in the worship of the Catholic Apostolic Church is very marked. This is evident in the following services: The office for Morning Prayer at 6 a.m., the office for Evening Prayer at 5 p.m., the Forenoon Service, the Litany, the Afternoon Service, the Shorter Morning Service, the Shorter Evening Service, the Churching of Women, the Administration of Holy Baptism and the Solemnisation of Marriage. Some additional and occasional prayers are taken from the same source.

Both 'Catholic Apostolic' and Anglican liturgies provide for daily services, morning and evening. But the Catholic Apostolic Morning Prayer diverges from the Prayer Book. From the Absolution are expunged the words, 'and hath given power, and commandment, to his Ministers, to declare and pronounce to his people, being penitent, the Absolution and Remission of their sins'. To the General Thanksgiving is added a sentence expressive of the millenarian expectations of the Church, 'looking for that blessed hope, and the glorious appearing of the great God and our Saviour Jesus Christ'. But the most significant addition is a prayer to be used by the Angel secretly at the Proposition of the Holy Sacrament. Provision is made for Communion after Morning Prayer, with the reserved elements. The prayer of Saint Chrysostom is included in the Forenoon Service, but is entitled, 'Concluding Prayer'. The Litany is enlarged with an intercession for the restored ministries of the Catholic Apostolic Church: 'That it may please Thee to send down Thy

The Holy Eucharist

The 'Catholic Apostolic Church' rite compared with the Greek rite, the Roman rite, and the English rite.

GREEK (Liturgy of St. Chrysostom).	ROMAN	ANGLICAN	THE APOSTLES'
Supplications and Prayers, with Antiphons.	Invocation. Psalm xliii. CONFESSION. ABSOLUTION.	Lord's Prayer. Prayer for Purity.	Invocation. CONFESSION. ABSOLUTION.
	Versicles. PRAYER OF ACCESS. Introit. KYRIE ELEISON.	Recital of Commandments, with KYRIE ELEISON. Prayer for King.	Versicles. PRAYER OF ACCESS.
TRISAGION.			KYRIE ELEISON.
	GLORIA IN EXCELSIS. COLLECT.	COLLECT.	GLORIA IN EXCELSIS. COLLECT.
Anthem (Prokeimenon) EPISTLE. GOSPEL.	EPISTLE. Anthem (Gradual) GOSPEL.	EPISTLE. GOSPEL. CREED.	EPISTLE. Anthem. GOSPEL.
	Sermon.	Sermon.	Homily.
Supplications and Prayers, and Expulsion of Catechumens.	CREED.	OFFERTORY.	CREED. OFFERTORY.
Prayers of the Faithful. Cherubic Hymn. Psalm li. BRINGING UP OF ELEMENTS, with Prayer of Oblation & Intercession.	Psalm xxvi. BRINGING UP OF ELEMENTS, with Prayer of Oblation.	BRINGING UP OF ELEMENTS, with Prayer of Oblation and Intercession.	Psalm xliii. BRINGING UP OF ELEMENTS, with Prayer of Oblation.

CREED.			
Salutation.	Salutation.	Exhortation.	Salutation.
'Lift up your hearts,' etc.	'Lift up your hearts,' etc.	Confession.	'Lift up your hearts,' etc.
PREFACE	PREFACE	Absolution.	PREFACE
(beginning, 'It is meet, right', etc., and ending, 'Therefore with angels', etc.)	(beginning, 'It is meet, right', etc., and ending, 'Therefore, with angels', etc.)	'Comfortable Words',	(beginning, 'It is meet, right', etc., and ending, 'Therefore with angels', etc.)
'HOLY, HOLY, HOLY', etc.	'HOLY, HOLY, HOLY', etc.	'Lift up your hearts', etc.	'HOLY, HOLY, HOLY', etc.
		PREFACE	
		(beginning, 'It is meet, right', etc., and ending, 'Therefore, with angels', etc.)	
		'HOLY, HOLY, HOLY', etc.	
			THE LORD'S PRAYER.
RECITAL OF INSTITUTION.	COMMEMORATION OF LIVING.	Prayer, 'We do not presume.'	{ INVOCATION OF H. SPIRIT. RECITAL OF INSTITUTION. PRAYER OF OBLATION. (After Consecration). }
PRAYER OF OBLATION.	RECITAL OF INSTITUTION.	RECITAL OF INSTITUTION.	
INVOCATION OF H. SPIRIT.	PRAYER OF OBLATION.		COMMEMORATIONS of Living and Departed.
COMMEMORATIONS of Living and Departed.	COMMEMORATION OF DEPARTED.		Prayer, 'Hasten, O God, the time'.
THE LORD'S PRAYER.	THE LORD'S PRAYER.		'We do not presume', etc.
The 'Prayer of Bowing Down.'	AGNUS DEI.		AGNUS DEI.
'Lord Jesu Christ', etc.			
SANCTA SANCTIS.	THE PEACE.		'Lord Jesu Christ', etc.
	Confession.		'O Holy Ghost'.
	Absolution.		SANCTA SANCTIS.
Anthem (Koinonikon)	COMMUNION.		THE PEACE.
COMMUNION.	Anthem (Post-Communion).	COMMUNION.	COMMUNION.
	Post-Communion Prayer.	THE LORD'S PRAYER.	Anthem (Post-Communion).
Post-Communion Prayer.	Reading of a Gospel.	Post-Communion Prayer.	Post-Communion Prayer.
		GLORIA IN EXCELSIS.	Te Deum.
Benediction.	Benediction.	Benediction.	Benediction.

heavenly grace upon apostles, prophets, evangelists, pastors, and teachers'. The address to the Trinity is omitted, as being a doctrine rather than a name of God. The service for the Churching of Women is taken intact from the Prayer Book but 'minister' is changed to 'priest', an indication of the high conception of the ministry held by this Church. The Administration of Holy Baptism is a more elaborate version of the Prayer Book service. The order for the Solemnisation of Matrimony closely follows the Anglican rite. But from the address is omitted the clause, 'like brute beasts that have no understanding', and the words beginning, 'It was ordained for a remedy against sin'. Provision is made for the celebration of the Holy Eucharist at the conclusion of a wedding, with a special commendation of the bride and bridegroom in the prayer of oblation, after consecration.

The Catechism is based on the Anglican, but is much elaborated as setting forth the teachings of the Catholic Apostolic Church.

CHAPTER XII

THE FREE CATHOLICS

THE rise and fall of the Society of Free Catholics is only a memory now. But in the years preceding and succeeding the First World War it excited much interest and some apprehension in the Free Churches. For a brief period it seemed as though a new spiritual force had arisen within Nonconformity, drawing much from an old and alien Catholic tradition, and heedless of the traditional groupings of Protestant denominationalism. The Church of England had had its Oxford movement. Now the Congregationalists were amazed to see the pageantry of the Mass in one of their London churches, and Birmingham Unitarians were astounded at the cross and altar lights in one of their ancient chapels.

It is probable that the Free Catholic movement, which had its origin in the libraries and studies of some gifted ministers, never had much chance of success in Nonconformity. It was an exotic growth, and as such it was soon recognised to be. Its meteoric rise was due to the fact that it had for apostles two of England's great preachers. Such men always attract adherents, disciples, and godly women not a few. But the disciples, though zealous, were never very considerable in number. A few Unitarian and Congregational ministers joined the society, and some Anglicans. Some of the Roman Catholic laity were sympathetic.

In their day the Free Catholics preached and wrote and made a stir. But the bulk of the laity remained unmoved. They preferred the denominations, churches and modes of worship to which they were accustomed. Some ministers, particularly among the Unitarians, began to suspect that with Catholic ritual was creeping in not a little Catholic intolerance. It was whispered that the Free Catholic leaders were cunningly wooing the leading pulpit appointments for their adherents. So far from the society becoming a unifying force among the Free Churches it was feared it might prove disruptive. It is possible that these fears were exaggerated but they were felt very deeply in some quarters. Yet it must be admitted that among Unitarians are devoted ministers who testify their lifelong indebtedness to the ideals and spiritual aspirations of the society.

The Free Catholic movement failed to capture historic Congregationalism or Unitarianism and perforce it had to die. But members of the society left behind a small but interesting legacy of prayer book experimentation.

It is not always possible to assess with certainty the formative causes of any movement. Men are influenced unconsciously by the habits of thought of their contemporaries. It has been said by some that the Free Catholics owed much to the liturgical activities of Dr. John Hunter and to the New Theology movement of Dr. R. J. Campbell. No doubt both Hunter and Campbell exercised an influence. But it was indirect rather than direct.

In 1905 Dr. John Hunter of Trinity Church, Glasgow, published *The Coming Church*, a plea for a Church simply Christian. This distinguished Congregationalist believed that the days of credal unity were over. Denominationalism had done all the good of which it was capable. It was time for it to go. Years before, in 1880, Hunter had published the well-known *Devotional Services for Public Worship*. This book he introduced to King's Weigh House, during his short London ministry. Hunter's successor at the King's Weigh House, Dr. W. E. Orchard, was not averse to his predecessor's book as a whole but he was unwilling to use the Communion office as too great a departure from historic form.

Some have asserted that the Free Catholic movement was the child of the New Theology. Strictly speaking this is not correct. The Free Catholic movement had none of the New Theology political interests. But it did cover to some extent a ground occupied by the defunct New Theology of which Dr. Orchard had been a leading exponent.

The Free Catholic movement had its origin in a plan of daily devotional exercises adopted by the Rev. J. M. Lloyd Thomas of Birmingham and another minister. At first it was a private devotional arrangement, but later it was extended to include others sympathetic with the idea. This little band formulated a constitution, and held a conference at the Old Meeting Church, Birmingham, which attracted considerable attention. Subsequently the movement was joined by Orchard. Those participating cultivated an intense devotional life, divorced from dogmatic thought. Some were inclined to Catholic sacramental practice. Others were not. This dichotomy persisted.

It is customary to regard Lloyd Thomas and Orchard as the chief exponents of Free Catholicism. But as time was to show Orchard was drawn irresistibly to the Roman tradition. After the 1914–18 war his views of the Eucharist tended increasingly towards transubstantiation. This separated him from the Free Catholics, especially as it induced him to accept orders from an irregular episcopal source. Orchard was ordained by Bishop Vernon Herford, who claimed to have been consecrated by the Metropolitan of the Jacobite Church of India.

In 1933 Orchard was received into the Roman Catholic Church. Before this time the Free Catholic Society had been disbanded. But Lloyd Thomas remained all his life a 'nonsubscriber' to creeds, and a Free Catholic in the tradition of his beloved Richard Baxter.

The liturgies published by Orchard and Lloyd Thomas were unofficial compilations, unsanctioned by any ecclesiastical body. But they became widely known. Years previous, when a Presbyterian minister at Enfield, Orchard had introduced a liturgical element into worship. This was, at first, a short opening prayer and general confession. Later he came to add some of Dr. Hunter's litanies. This experimentation was important since it was done without any attempt at concealment. Not only the minister but the congregation adopted the liturgical form. In London, at the King's Weigh House, Orchard became nominally a Congregationalist. He retained his predecessor's *Devotional Services* omitting the Communion Service. For this he used a form of his own inspired by the Book of Common Prayer.

In 1919 he published *The Order of Divine Service for Public Worship*. A revised edition appeared in 1926. *Divine Service* borrowed the plan of *Devotional Services* in having ten services for Sundays, extra litanies, and services for Special Feasts such as Christmas and Easter. But the Eucharist, later revised for the final edition, was based on Egyptian, Greek and

Roman liturgies, with very little material from the Anglican. The ceremonial was Roman.

Lloyd Thomas did much to bring together a wealth of liturgical tradition in his *Free Church Book of Common Prayer* issued in 1929. The book was compiled for use in the Old Meeting House, Birmingham. It had no specific connection with the Free Catholic movement. But the Free and Catholic character of the liturgy is apparent at once. It provides ten orders of Sunday worship. Of these two are slight modifications of Anglican Morning and Evening Prayer. It includes services of Prime and Compline, and a Sunday morning order designed for the use of non-Christian theists, with prayers from the Jewish liturgy. A Free order of worship is appended. In accordance with the early usage of the Christian church the Apostles' and the Nicene Creeds are not incorporated in any service. But they are printed in the appendix.

Many collects and prayers are inserted for the Church year and for diverse occasions. The invitation to Communion states that this sacrament of the Lord is open to all. The Eucharistic Prayer includes the epiclesis and institution. A prayer of Oblation follows. Provision is made for the reservation of the sacrament for the Communion of the Sick. Not always is it realised that even Calvin was prepared to tolerate reservation for this purpose. Many Church of Scotland clergymen reserve the sacrament for sick parishioners.

In the Baptismal office the minister addresses both parents and godparents. It is their duty to undertake for the child the baptismal vows. In the Confirmation Service the laying on of hands is by the minister. Provision is made for communion after the Solemnisation of Marriage.

A Free Church book of Common Prayer is derived from many sources. But the influence of the Prayer Book, Sadler and Martineau's *Common Prayer for Christian Worship*, Hunter's *Devotional Services* and Orchard's *Divine Service* is apparent.

The book met with extraordinary success on first appearance. It was greeted with eulogistic reviews on the Continent, and in the United States, Canada, and Australia. *The British Weekly* and *The Christian World* gave it a blessing. Within a fortnight the first edition was exhausted. In rushing haste, a second edition was printed. But already it was doomed. Ugly rumours began to spread. Free Churchmen suspected they had been tricked into thinking that the book was an unofficial product of their own representatives. This was a singular misapprehension since the editor had stated in his foreword that the book was without official sanction. 'It created quite a scare on publication' wrote Dr. Orchard, 'because it was taken to be an official publication of the Free Churches in some capacity; and was as swiftly disowned.' For the title was misleading. The term 'Free Church' had come to mean one of the Dissenting Churches in England. But Lloyd Thomas interpreted 'Free Church' as something more inclusive than Dissent. Was not the Episcopal Church itself a Dissenting Church in Scotland?

It was not long before the discovery was made that the book was the work of a Free Catholic, and Free Churchmen concluded that the absence of the editor's name was a sinister device to deceive.

Years afterwards Mr. Lloyd Thomas assured the writer that no such deception had been intended. He had sought to avoid any kudos from the publication of a work for which he had refused to receive a penny, and which he had compiled to the glory of God. In a letter he wrote: 'Who was I to let my name be thrust upon it? What better thing could I do in this connection than to offer it humbly, and free from personal advertisement, to our Blessed Lord Jesus Christ?'

Despite the outburst *A Free Church Book of Common Prayer* continued to be valued as a treasury of praise and prayer by many ministers. In particular the American Lutherans drew much from this source. During the controversies connected with the Deposited Book there were extreme Anglo-Catholics who went so far as to declare that were the bishops to sanction the form of Eucharist printed in *A Free Church Book of Common Prayer* they would be satisfied.

Seldom have the liturgies of Hunter, Orchard or Lloyd Thomas been adopted by congregations. But they bear witness to that growing interest in liturgical worship that is one of the most surprising features of modern Nonconformity. Free Churchmen as well as High Churchmen have sought the beauty of holiness. With equal devotion, they have gone on quest for the Grail.

RETROSPECT

THIS book is an attempt to describe the long and virile Prayer Book tradition in the Free Churches. No doubt the liturgical achievements of the denominations are unequal. But behind the craftsmanship or genius of the prayer-book maker is a perennial theology valid for all sorts and conditions of men. The human soul still seeks the solace and grace of its Maker. Our cry today is but an echo from the far-off days of the Shepherd King. 'In my distress I called upon the Lord, and cried to my God: and He did hear my voice out of His temple, and my cry did enter into His ears.'

There is thus behind all liturgiology an essential unity. Men and women forget sectarian differences in an act of common devotion. They are made one by the One they adore.

Increasingly the Free Churches are discovering a unity among themselves that is spiritual and ultra-denominational. Nor is this unity of prayer and praise confined to themselves. They are experiencing a closer sense of kinship with the Church of England, and a more perfect understanding of the Body of Christ.

Something of this at least was anticipated by the distinguished Congregationalist, Dr. John Hunter, in these words: 'Emerson, writing of the results of the division of labour, says that if we look around we see here an arm, there a foot, in one place a head, and in another a hand, but nowhere a complete man. It is the same with the ideal of the Church. One part or side of it we find represented by the Roman Catholics, other parts or sides by Lutherans, Anglicans, Presbyterians, Methodists, Independents, Unitarians, Quakers, Moravians, Plymouth Brethren, Swedenborgians. The true Catholic Church will seek to take into itself all the good elements, all the helpful usages and customs, which are to be found in all the Churches and sects, and seek to make them part of its own order and life.

Of those who argue for separation and division and the exalting and magnifying of differences, it will ask: 'Is Christ divided?' It may be that the Way of Reunion will be by common prayer.

BIBLIOGRAPHY

Bod. = Bodleian Library, Oxford.
B.M. = British Museum.
B.H. = Bible House, London. (British and Foreign Bible Society)
J.R. = John Rylands Library, Manchester.

THE CHURCH OF ENGLAND

SOURCES

The following are Puritan revisions of the Sixteenth and Seventeenth Centuries.

The Order of Common Prayer. The ministration of Christ's holy Sacraments and of Christian discipline used in the English congregation at Frankfurt (1555). (Papers of Dean T. Sampson, 1564–75), B.M.

Puritan editions of the Book of Common Prayer bound with Geneva Bibles.

1578. J.R., i.e. The Bible with Annotations whereunto is added the Psalter of the common translation agreeing with The Book of Common Prayer (*The Book of Common Prayer and Administration of the Sacraments*). Christopher Barker, London, 1578.

1579   B.H.
1579   B.H.
1580   B.H.
1580   B.H.
1581   B.H.
1582   Bod.
1583   B.M.
1585   B.H.
1589   (Reference made by Procter and Frere, *A History of the Book of Common Prayer*).
1592   B.H.
1592   J.R. (Very incomplete. Communion office not included).
1594? J.R. (Incorporated with 1598 Geneva Bible).
1596   B.H.
1597   Bod.

1597 B.M.
1603 B.H.
1606 B.H.
1607 J.R.
1607 B.H. (Incorporated with 1610 Geneva Bible).
1608 J.R.
1611 B.H. (Incorporated with 1612 Geneva Bible).
1613? B.H. (Authorised B.C.P. with Geneva New Testament).
1614 B.H.
1614 B.H. (Incorporated with 1615 Geneva Bible).
1615 B.H.
1616 B.H.
1630 Bod.

The Revised Liturgy of 1689, being the Book of Common Prayer, interleaved with the alterations prepared for Convocation by the Royal Commissioners, edited by John Taylor. London, 1855.

SECONDARY WORKS

The Second Prayer Book of King Edward VI, edited by H. J. Wotherspoon. Edinburgh, 1905.

A Brief Discourse of the Troubles begun at Frankfort in the year 1554, about the Book of Common Prayer and ceremonies. London, 1846 edition.

The Liturgy of Compromise by George W. Sprott. Edinburgh, 1905.

The Prayer Book of Queen Elizabeth (Ancient and Modern Library of Theological Literature).

Elizabethan Liturgical Services, edited by W. K. Clay, 1847.

The Prayer Book Dictionary, edited by Harford and Stevenson.

The Annotated Book of Common Prayer by J. H. Blunt. London, 1876.

The Prayer Book; its History, Language, and Contents by Evan Daniel. London.

A New History of the Book of Common Prayer by Procter and Frere. London, 1925 edition.

A History of the Book of Common Prayer by Thomas Lathbury. 1858.

The History of the Reformation of the Church of England by Peter Heylyn. 3rd edition. London, 1674.

The Bibles of England by Andrew Edgar. London, 1899.

The Reign of Elizabeth by J. B. Black. Oxford, 1936.

History of the Puritans by Daniel Neal. London, 1822.

A Short History of Puritanism by James Heron. Edinburgh, 1908.

The Presbyterian Movement in the reign of Queen Elizabeth by R. G. Usher. Camden Society, 1905.

The History of the Life and Acts of Edmund Grindal by John Strype.

G 179

Thomas Cartwright and Elizabethan Puritanism, 1535–1603 by Rev. A. F. Scott Pearson.
Aerius Redivivus or the History of the Presbyterians by Peter Heylyn. 2nd edition. London, 1672.
Notable Editions of the Prayer Book by J. F. Gerrard. Wigan, 1949.
History of the Convocation of the Church of England by Thomas Lathbury, 1842.
Statutes and Constitutional Documents, 1558–1625 by G. W. Prothero. Oxford, 1913.
Notitia Eucharistica by W. E. Scudamore. London, 2nd edition, 1876.
Edmund Grindal (1519?–1583). D.N.B.
William Whittingham (1524?–1579). D.N.B.
Christopher Barker (1529?–1599). D.N.B.
John Whitgift (1530?–1604). D.N.B.
Richard Jugge (1531–1577). D.N.B.
Richard Bancroft (1544–1610). D.N.B.
James Usher (1581–1656). D.N.B.

THE METHODISTS

The following editions of the 'Abridgement' were published for the United States and the Colonies:

The Sunday Service of the Methodists in North America. With other Occasional Services. London: Printed in the year MDCCLXXXIV. (Twenty-three copies of this edition have been discovered, and all are in the United States or Canada. One well-known copy is in the Rose Memorial Library, Drew University, New Jersey, U.S.A.) In Morning and Evening Prayer, petitions are offered for the Supreme Rulers of these United States. There are only twenty-four Articles of Religion. Another edition was published in 1784, with a preface dated Bristol, September 9.

The Sunday Service of the Methodists in the United States of America. With other Occasional Services, 1784. (Copy in Methodist Book Room, City Road, London.)

The Sunday Service of the Methodists in the United States of America. With other Occasional Services. London: Printed by Frys and Couchman, Worship Street, Upper Moorfields, 1786. (Copy in Didsbury College, Bristol.)

The Sunday Service of the Methodists in His Majesty's Dominions. With other Occasional Services. London: Printed by Frys and Couchman, Worship Street, Upper Moorfields, 1786. (Copy in the possession of the Rev. John J. Perry.)

Another edition, 1788.

Fourth edition, 1792.

Many subsequent editions.

The Sunday Service of the Methodists in the United States of America. With other Occasional Services. Fourth edition. London: Printed in the year MDCCXC. (Copy in the library of Emory University, Georgia, U.S.A., and in the Methodist Book Room, City Road, London.)

The following editions of the 'Abridgement' were published for Great Britain:

The Sunday Service of the Methodists, with other Occasional Services. Printed by Frys and Couchman, Worship Street, Upper Moorfields. London, 1786. J.R.

The Sunday Service of the Methodists. With other Occasional Services. London: printed in the year 1788. B.M. (Titles of four collects in morning service omitted.)

The Sunday Service of the Methodists. With other Occasional Services. Fourth edition. London, 1792. B.M. (Preface not dated. Twenty-five Articles of Religion; 23rd Article being, 'Of the Rulers of the British Dominions'.)

The Sunday Service of the Methodists late in Connexion with the Rev. John Wesley, M.A. With other Occasional Services. Fifth edition. London: Conference Office, Cordeux, 1816.

Sixth edition, 1816 ⎱ Slight changes were made in these, and
Seventh edition, 1817 ⎰ succeeding editions.

The Catalogue of these editions by the Rev. Wesley F. Swift appears in the *Proceedings of the Wesley Historical Society* (March, 1958).

J.R.	= John Rylands Library, Manchester.
E.P.	= Epworth Press Library.
F.B.	= Dr. Frank Baker.
O.A.B.	= Dr. Oliver A. Beckerlegge.
L.	= Wesley College, Leeds.
W.F.S.	= Rev. Wesley F. Swift.
J.C.B.	= Rev. John C. Bowmer.
W.R.B.	= Mr. W. R. Batty (Southport).

1817 (Sixth edition)	J.R.	1859	E.P.
1819 (seventh edition)	E.P.	1860	E.P.
1825 (12mo)	E.P.	1861	W.R.B.
1825 (24mo)	W.F.S.	1863	W.F.S.
1826	E.P.	1873	E.P.

1834	E.P.	1876			J.C.B.
1837	E.P.	1878			F.B.
1838	E.P.	N.D. (1):	c. 1846–60	E.P.
1841	E.P.	N.D. (2):	c. 1846–60	E.P.
1842	F.B.	N.D. (3):	c. 1846–60	E.P.
1846	E.P.	N.D. (4):	c. 1865	E.P.
1849	E.P.	N.D. (5):	c. 1901	W.F.S.
1852	W.F.S.	N.D. (6):	c. 1902	F.B.
1857	F.B.	N.D. (7):	c. 1910	E.P.

In addition to the above, all of which bear the title, *The Sunday Service of the Methodists,* there are other service books with the title, *Order of Administration of the Sacraments and other Services, for the Use of the People called Methodists,* which in their reduced contents correspond roughly to the present *Shorter Book of Offices.*

1839	E.P.	1858	E.P.	1873	J.C.B.
1848	J.C.B.	1863	O.A.B.	1875	E.P.
1852	W.F.S.	1864	E.P.	1878	J.C.B.
1856	E.P.	1865	J.C.B.	1879	E.P.
1857	E.P.	1867	L.	1881	E.P.

The following Wesleyan Methodist prayer books have also been published:

Forms of Common Prayer for those who attend in Bethesda Chapel, Dublin (1786).
    N.B. The editor, Edward Smyth, had been a clergyman of the Church of Ireland. See writer's article in the *Proceedings of the Wesley Historical Society,* December 1958.
Order of Administration of the Lord's Supper and Baptism; the Forms of Solemnisation of Matrimony, and of the Burial of the Dead; together with the Ordination Service: as used by all Wesleyan Methodists. London, 1848. B.M.
Canticles and Services used at the Wesleyan Chapel, Mornington Road, Southport. Southport, 1867. B.M.
The Book of Public Prayers and Services for the use of the People called Methodists. London, 1882, 1883. B.M.
Service Book: including Chants and Hymns with Devotional and Sacramental Services, for use in Wesleyan-Methodist Congregations. Southport, 1889. B.M.
Order of Sabbath Services used in the Longsight Wesleyan Methodist Circuit, Manchester. Manchester, 1899. B.M.
Morning Service and Holy Communion (Trinity Methodist Church, Southport).

Morning Service (for The Methodist Centenary Church, St. Stephen's Green, Dublin), 1938. Liturgical worship has continued in this congregation since 1788. It is the only church in Irish Methodism to use a B.C.P. revision.

The following service books have been issued by other Methodist Communions:

PRIMITIVE METHODISTS

Forms for the Administration of Baptism; the Solemnisation of Matrimony; Maternal thanksgiving after childbirth; Administration of the Lord's Supper; renewing our Covenant with God; and for the Burial of the Dead. London, 1860. B.M.
Order of Administration of Baptism and other Services for the use of the Primitive Methodists. London.

BIBLE CHRISTIAN CHURCH

Book of Services for the use of the Bible Christian Church. New edition. London, 1903.

UNITED METHODIST FREE CHURCHES

Book of Services for the use of the United Methodist Free Churches, London.

UNITED METHODIST CHURCH

Book of Services for the use of the United Methodist Church, prepared by direction of the Conference. London, 1913.
Sanctuary Worship: Responsive Services, Sentences and Prayers, arranged for Public Worship by the Rev. Ernest F. H. Capey (1916).

The following liturgies have been sanctioned by the Conference of the Methodist Church:

Divine Worship. Approved by the Conference for optional use in Methodist Churches. London, 1935.
The Book of Offices being the Orders of Service authorised for use in the Methodist Church. London, 1936.

SECONDARY WORKS

The Letters of the Rev. John Wesley. Edited by John Telford.

The Journal of the Rev. John Wesley. Standard edition, edited by N. Curnock.

Son to Susanna by G. Elsie Harrison. 1937.

'The Separation of Methodism from the Church of England' by A. W. Harrison. (Wesley Historical Society Lecture, No. 11.) 1945.

'John Wesley's Lectionary' by Wesley F. Swift (*The London Quarterly and Holborn Review*, Oct., 1958).

'The Sunday Service of the Methodists' by J. Hamby Barton. (*Proceedings of the Wesley Historical Society*, March, 1960).

More about the Early Methodist People by Leslie F. Church. London, 1949.

The Story of Methodism. An Essay by H. B. Workman.

The Genius of Methodism. An Essay by A. S. Peake.

Vital Elements of Public Worship by J. E. Rattenbury. London, 1936.

The Rites and Ritual of Episcopal Methodism by Nolan B. Harmon, Jn. U.S.A., 1926.

'Methodism and the Book of Common Prayer' by Wesley F. Swift. (*Proceedings of the Wesley Historical Society.* June, 1949.)

'Green's Wesley Bibliography' by Richard Green. (*Proceedings of the Wesley Historical Society.* Vol. 3, p. 130.)

'Sources of Wesley's Revision of the Prayer Book in 1784-8' by Frederick Hunter. (*Proceedings of the Wesley Historical Society.* Vol. XXIII, pp. 123-33.)

'United Methodism in the Evolution of the Methodist Church' by Albert Hearn. (*Proceedings of the Wesley Historical Society.* September, 1950.)

'The Sunday Service of the Methodists: A Study of Nineteenth-century Liturgy' by Wesley F. Swift. (*Proceedings of the Wesley Historical Society.* March, 1958; June, 1958).

'The Sunday Service of the Methodists' by Wesley F. Swift. (*Proceedings of the Wesley Historical Society.* March, 1953.)

Worship and Theology in England, Vol. 3 by Horton Davies. (Quoted by kind permission Princeton University Press.)

THE COUNTESS OF HUNTINGDON'S CONNEXION

SOURCES

Amended copies of the Book of Common Prayer (unpublished).

The Free Church Prayer Book, being the Public Services of the Book of Common Prayer of the Established Church of England, revised and enlarged by the Rev. James Mountain. London, 1897, B.M.

SECONDARY WORKS

'The Countess of Huntingdon' by F. F. Bretherton. London, 1940.
(Wesley Historical Society Lecture, No. 6.)

THE FREE CHURCH OF ENGLAND AND THE REFORMED EPISCOPAL CHURCH

SOURCES

*The Book of Common Prayer as revised and proposed to the use of the
Protestant Episcopal Church* (i.e. of America), 1785.
N.B. This is the 'Proposed Book' of the Protestant Episcopal
Church of America, republished in 1873 (Bishop Vaughan's
collection).
The Book of Common Prayer of the Reformed Episcopal Church (*i.e.* of
America). Philadelphia, U.S.A., 1874.
*The Book of Common Prayer according to the use of the Reformed
Episcopal Church in the United Kingdom, otherwise called the Reformed
Church of England.* London, 1879.
*The Book of Common Prayer revised according to the use of the Free Church
of England.* London, 1876.
The Book of Common Prayer revised. (Special edition issued by the
Prayer Book Revision Society, 'for the use of the Free Church of
England'). London, 1876.
*The Book of Common Prayer for use in the Free Church of England, otherwise
called the Reformed Episcopal Church in the United Kingdom of Great
Britain and Ireland.* London, 1936.

SECONDARY WORKS

*A History of the Free Church of England otherwise called the Reformed
Episcopal Church* by F. Vaughan. Bath, 1936.
Hastings' *Encyclopaedia of Religion and Ethics*, Vol. X (article by
C. H. Jones).
The Free Church of England: Its Doctrines and Ecclesiastical Polity by
George Hugh Jones.
Are there Romanising Germs in the Prayer Book? by F. S. Rising. Phila-
delphia, U.S.A., 1883. (N.B. This tract is very rare. A copy is in
the possession of Bishop Higgins, of Philadelphia, U.S.A.)
Events leading to the formation of the Reformed Episcopal Church by D. O.
Kellog. New York, 1893.
*The Origin, Orders, Organisation, and worship of the Reformed Episcopal
Church in the United Kingdom* by Philip Eldridge.
The Mission of our Church by Robert L. Rudolph.

THE MORAVIANS

SOURCES

Acta Fratrum Unitatis in Anglia. London, MDCCXLIX. This includes *The Church Litany of the Brethren; used in the Brethren's Communities, and also in all the places where there are regulated Congregations; together with the Ritual of the Synod and the Convocation House.*
Note. The *Acta Fratrum* was issued by Zinzendorf, on the advice of Wilson, Bishop of Sodor and Man. The *Church Litany* had been revised by Sherlock, Bishop of London.

A Collection of Hymns for the use of the Protestant Church of the United Brethren. London, 1789. B.M.

A Collection of Hymns, for the use of the Protestant Church of the United Brethren. Revised and enlarged. (Preceded by the Liturgy.) Bath, 1801. B.M.

A Collection of Hymns, for the use of the Protestant Church of the United Brethren. New and revised edition. (Preceded by the Liturgy.) Manchester, 1809. B.M.

A Collection of Hymns, for the use of the Protestant Church of the United Brethren. New and revised edition. (Preceded by the Liturgy.) Ashton-under-Lyne, 1826. B.M.

Hymns for the use of the Protestant Church of the United Brethren. A new edition. (Preceded by the Liturgy.) London, 1836. B.M.

Liturgy and Hymns for the use of the Protestant Church of the United Brethren. A new edition. London, 1838. B.M.

Liturgy and Hymns for the use of the Protestant Church of the United Brethren. A new edition. London, 1844. B.M.

Liturgy and Hymns for use of the Protestant Church of the United Brethren, or Unitas Fratrum. A new and revised edition. London, 1849. B.M.

Liturgy and Hymns for the use of the Protestant Church of the United Brethren, or Unitas Fratrum. A new and revised edition. London, 1854. B.M.

Liturgy and Hymns for the use of the Protestant Church of the United Brethren, or Unitas Fratrum. A new and revised edition. London, 1869. B.M.

Liturgy and Hymns for the use of the Protestant Church of the United Brethren, or Unitas Fratrum. A new and revised edition. London, 1886.

The Liturgy and Hymns authorised for use in the Moravian Church (Unitas Fratrum) in Great Britain and Ireland. London, 1911 (1912).

The Moravian Liturgy, O.U.P., 1960.

Supplement to the Moravian Hymn Book Edition 1911. London, 1940.

Two Specimen *Odes* for 1839 and 1855.

Liturgic Hymns of the United Brethren. Revised edition. London, 1864. Note. Some of these liturgies, together with a copy of the very rare *Acta Fratrum Unitatis in Anglia* were lent to the writer by the late Rev. H. Hassall, Principal of Fairfield College, Manchester. With great kindness, the Principal supplied particulars of the earlier liturgical activities of the United Brethren. These are to be found only in inaccessible books and periodicals.

SECONDARY WORKS

A History of the Moravian Church by J. E. Hutton. Second edition, revised and enlarged. London, 1909.
History of the Moravian Church by Edward Langton. London, 1956.
Zinzendorf. The Ecumenical Pioneer by A. J. Lewis. S.C.M., 1962.

THE CONGREGATIONALISTS

SOURCES

The Congregational Service Book: A form of public worship designed for the use of the Independent and other Nonconformist Bodies in Great Britain. London, 1847. B.M.
A Biblical Liturgy for the use of Evangelical Churches and Homes. Compiled by the Rev. David Thomas. London, 1856. B.M.
Liturgies for Divine Worship. London, c. 1860.
Free Church Service Book. Preface by Newman Hall. London, 1867. B.M.
A Form of Morning and Evening Service for the use of Free Churches. Manchester, 1869.
Forms submitted for the use of Nonconformist Churches. 1870. B.M.
The Liturgy of the Church of England (abridged) by David Thomas. 1874. B.M.
Devotional Services for Public Worship by John Hunter, 1880. First issue of revised edition, 1901. Reprinted, 1903, 1915, 1920, 1924, 1930, 1936, 1943.
Let us Pray. A handbook of selected collects, and forms of prayer for the use of Free Churches. Arranged by C. Silvester Horne and T. Herbert Darlow. Second edition, 1897.
Devotional Services for use in Mill Hill Chapel. 1895.
Intercessory Services for aid in Public Worship by P. T. Forsyth. Manchester, 1896.
Prayer and Praise. (E. D. Cecil.) 1914.
N.B. This liturgy was compiled for Penge Congregational Church.
Orders of Worship by H. E. Brierley. Third edition. 1950.
N.B. This liturgy was compiled for Immanuel Church, Southborne, Bournemouth.

Typed litanies for the Purley Church by Arthur Pringle.
Intercession Services for Congregational use in public worship by G. H. Russell. Matlock, 1923.
The Rodborough Bede Book.
    N.B. This liturgy was privately printed for the Rev. C. E. Watson of Rodborough, Stroud.
Book of Congregational Worship. Edinburgh, 1920.
A Manual for Ministers. London, 1936.
Services for Derby Street Congregational Church, Bolton, by R. Lawrence Jones, 1943.
Responsals. Acts of Prayer and Worship for Congregational Use by E. R. Micklem and Irene M. Shewell Cooper. London, 1947.
A Book of Public Worship. Compiled for the use of Congregationalists. Oxford, 1948, 1949.
Prayers and Services for Christian Festivals by James M. Todd. Oxford, 1951.
A Book of Services and Prayers. London, 1959.

SECONDARY WORKS

Essays Congregational and Catholic. Edited by A. Peel. London, 1931.
The Story of Congregationalism. An Essay by Albert Peel.
Congregationalism. An Essay by J. Vernon Bartlet.
David Thomas (1813–94). D.N.B.
Christopher Newman Hall (1816–1902). D.N.B.
Correspondence with the Rev. J. M. Todd, M.A.; and the Rev. Dr. J. Marsh, Principal of Mansfield College, Oxford.

THE BAPTISTS

SOURCES

Services for Public Worship, prepared by Henry Bonner. Revised edition, 1900. Birmingham. (First published *c.* 1890.)
The Baptist Church Hymnal. (The edition of 1900.) London.
A Manual for Free Church Ministers. London. Date uncertain. Before 1914.
Come, Let Us Worship. A Book of Common Worship for use in Free Churches. London, 1930. Edited by Frederick C. Spurr.
The Call to Worship, by D. Tait Patterson, 1930, 1931, 1938 (revised), 1947 (enlarged).
A Minister's Manual, arranged by M. E. Aubrey. London, 1927, 1946, 1952.
Readings for Worship by J. I. Jones. London, 1937.

SECONDARY WORKS

The Works of John Smyth. Edited by W. T. Whitley. Vol. I. Cambridge University Press, 1915.

History of British Baptists by W. T. Whitley. 1923.

The Life and Faith of the Baptists by H. Wheeler Robinson. London, 1927.

Free Churchmanship in England (1870–1940) by John W. Grant. London, 1955.

History of Victoria Road Church, Leicester. 1946.

CHURCHES OF CHRIST

Churches of Christ Scripture Readings. Berean Press, Birmingham, 1963.

Studies on Baptism. Edited by James Gray. Berean Press, Birmingham, 1959.

What Churches of Christ Stand For by William Robinson. Berean Press, Birmingham, 1959.

Declaration and Address by Thomas Campbell, with an introduction by William Robinson. Berean Press, Birmingham, 1959. (First published 1809.)

The Christian System in reference to the Union of Christians and Restoration of Primitive Christianity by A. Campbell. Reprinted by the Publishing Committee of Churches of Christ, Birmingham. (First published 1835.)

Towards Christian Union by Members of the Union Committee of Churches of Christ. Edited by James Gray, 1960.

The Shattered Cross. The Many Churches and the One Church by William Robinson. Berean Press, Birmingham, 1945.

THE NEW CHURCH

SOURCES

Note. Most of these liturgies are to be found in the library of the Swedenborg Society, 20 Bloomsbury Way, London, W.C.1.

The Liturgy of the New Church signified by the New Jerusalem in the Revelation. Printed and sold by R. Hindmarsh, London. Third edition, 1790. Fourth edition, 1791. Fifth edition, 1797. Bod.

The Liturgy of the Lord's New Church (signified by the New Jerusalem in the Revelation) formed upon the plan of that of the Church of England. Manchester, MDCCXCIII.

The Order of Worship of the Society of the New Church, meeting in Red Cross Street, Near Barbican, London, 1794. B.M.

The Liturgy of the New Church, as used in York Street Chapel, St. James's Square, Westminster. 1800. Bod.

The Liturgy of the New Church, signified by the New Jerusalem in the Revelation. London, 1802, 1805.

Rites and Ceremonies for the use of The Lord's Church, signified by the New Jerusalem in the Revelation. London, 1807.

The Liturgy of the New Church, with Rites and Ceremonies. London, 1810 (two editions).

N.B. This liturgy is almost identical with *The Liturgy of the New Church, signified by the New Jerusalem, in the Revelation.* London, 1802, 1805.

The Liturgy of the New Church, signified by the New Jerusalem in the Apocalypse. Manchester, A.D. 1813. Being the 57th year of the New Jerusalem.

N.B. A very similar edition was printed, but date unknown.

An Outline of the Form of Worship used in St. George's Chapel, Near Oldham Road, Manchester. Manchester, 1819.

The Liturgy of the New Church, signified by the New Jerusalem in the Revelation. Prepared by order of the General Conference. London, 1828, 1831, 1852 (Fifth edition).

A Liturgy from the Divine Word. London. Second edition, 1858.

The Liturgy used by the society of the New Church (signified by 'The New Jerusalem' in the Revelation) in Argyle Square Church, King's Cross, London. London, 1859, 1863.

Liturgy for the New Church signified by the New Jerusalem in the Revelation. London, 1875.

Liturgy for the New Church signified by the New Jerusalem in the Revelation. London, 1903, 1912.

Liturgy for the New Church compiled by order of the General Conference of the New Church. London, 1925.

SECONDARY WORKS

Arcana Coelestia. The first volume was published by Emanuel Swedenborg in 1749. It is an exposition of the spiritual sense of Genesis and Exodus. (Everyman Library)

Heaven and Hell. This book, *De Coelo et ejus Mirabilibus et de Inferno,* is the best known of Swedenborg's works.

Conjugal Love. This book, *Deliciae Sapientiae de Amore Conjugiali,* is the first revelatory work to which Swedenborg attached his name. 1768.

The True Christian Religion. This book, *Vera Christiana Religio,* is held by many non-Swedenborgians to be the finest of Swedenborg's writings. 1771.

A New-Church Manual by H. Gordon Drummond.
Swedenborg. Life and Teaching by G. Trobridge. Published by the
Swedenborg Society. London, 1935.
Encyclopaedia of Religion and Ethics, Vol. 12. Article by L. B. De
Beaumont.
'Swedenborg; or the Mystic', in *Representative Men* by Ralph Waldo
Emerson.
Thomas Hartley (1709–1784). D.N.B.
John Clowes (1743–1831). D.N.B.
Joseph Proud (1745–1826). D.N.B.
Robert Hindmarsh (1759–1835). D.N.B.
William Cowherd (1763–1816). D.N.B.
Correspondence with the Rev. Dennis Duckworth of the New
Church College, Woodford Green, Essex.

THE CATHOLIC APOSTOLIC CHURCH

SOURCES

The Liturgy and other Divine Offices of the Church. 1843, 1847, 1851,
1853, 1856, 1863, 1869, 1880.
N.B. Additional material is to be found in each succeeding
edition. There were eight editions in all. Reprints only have been
issued since 1880.

SECONDARY WORKS

*The History and Claims of the Body of Christians known as the 'Catholic
Apostolic Church'* by the late Rev. W. W. Andrews. Reprinted from
the *Bibliotheca Sacra* for January and April, 1866. (Sixth edition,
1945.)
The Theological Review, Vol. iii, Nos. XII–XV (1866).
'The Development of the Liturgy and the Origin of the Prayers.'
Two discourses delivered recently in the Southwark Church.
January, 1950.
Correspondence with Mr. Christopher B. Heath. He was one of the
very few surviving priests. He died in 1961.

THE FREE CATHOLICS

SOURCES

The Order of Divine Service for Public Worship. (1919)
N.B. A revised edition was published by Dr. Orchard in 1926.

BIBLIOGRAPHY

A Free Church Book of Common Prayer. (1929)
The Sacrament of Holy Communion (compiled by John Stone Burgess, Minister of Flowery Field Church, Hyde (1909–49). Burgess was for years an official of the Free Catholic Society. The church is traditionally Unitarian).

SECONDARY WORKS

'The Free Catholic Movement' (article by Bruce Findlow in the *Transactions of the Unitarian Historical Society,* October, 1958).
From Faith to Faith by W. E. Orchard. 1933.
Correspondence with the Rev. W. E. Orchard, D.D., the Rev. J. M. Lloyd Thomas, and the Rev. Stanley Mossop.

INDEX OF PERSONS

PRAYER BOOK INDEX

PRAYER BOOK INDEX

INDEX OF PLACES

Printed in the United Kingdom
by Lightning Source UK Ltd.
103153UKS00002B/18